Designed and Edited by Hal Schuster

OTHER PIONEER BOOKS

•THE MAGICAL MICHAEL JACKSON
Edited by Hal Schuster. March, 1990. $9.95, ISBN#1-55698-235-6
•FISTS OF FURY: THE FILMS OF BRUCE LEE
Written by Edward Gross. March, 1990. $14.95, ISBN #1-55698-233-X
•WHO WAS THAT MASKED MAN?
Written by James Van Hise. March, 1990. $14.95, ISBN #1-55698-227-5
•PAUL MCCARTNEY: 20 YEARS ON HIS OWN
Written by Edward Gross. February, 1990. $9.95, ISBN #1-55698-263-1
•THE DARK SHADOWS TRIBUTE BOOK
Written by Edward Gross and James Van Hise. February, 1990. $14.95, ISBN#1-55698-234-8
•THE UNOFFICIAL TALE OF BEAUTY AND THE BEAST, 2nd Edition
Written by Edward Gross. $14.95, 164 pages, ISBN #1-55698-261-5
•TREK: THE LOST YEARS
Written by Edward Gross. $12.95, 128 pages, ISBN #1-55698-220-8
•THE TREK ENCYCLOPEDIA
Written by John Peel. $19.95, 368 pages, ISBN#1-55698-205-4
•HOW TO DRAW ART FOR COMIC BOOKS
Written by James Van Hise. $14.95, 160 pages, ISBN#1-55698-254-2
•THE TREK CREW BOOK
Written by James Van Hise. $9.95, 112 pages, ISBN#1-55698-256-9
•THE OFFICIAL PHANTOM SUNDAYS
Written by Lee Falk. $14.95, 128 pages, ISBN#1-55698-250-X
•BLONDIE & DAGWOOD: AMERICA'S FAVORITE FAMILY
Written by Dean Young. $6.95, 132 pages, ISBN#1-55698-222-4
•THE DOCTOR AND THE ENTERPRISE
Written by Jean Airey. $9.95, 136 pages, ISBN#1-55698-218-6
•THE MAKING OF THE NEXT GENERATION
Written by Edward Gross. $14.95, 128 pages, ISBN#1-55698-219-4
•THE MANDRAKE SUNDAYS
Written by Lee Falk. $12.95, 104 pages, ISBN#1-55698-216-X
•BATMANIA
Written by James Van Hise. $14.95, 176 pages, ISBN#1-55698-252-6
•GUNSMOKE
Written by John Peel. $14.95, 204 pages, ISBN#1-55698-221-6
•ELVIS-THE MOVIES: THE MAGIC LIVES ON
Written by Hal Schuster. $14.95, ISBN#1-55698-223-2
•STILL ODD AFTER ALL THESE YEARS: ODD COUPLE COMPANION.
Written by Edward Gross. $12.95, 132 pages, ISBN#1-55698-224-0
•SECRET FILE: THE UNOFFICIAL MAKING OF A WISEGUY
Written by Edward Gross. $14.95, 164 pages, ISBN#1-55698-261-5

DARK SHADOWS TRIBUTE

Edward Gross and James Van Hise

PIONEER BOOKS, INC.   LAS VEGAS, NEVADA

Library of Congress Cataloging-in-Publication Data
James Van Hise, 1949— and Edward Gross, 1960—
    Dark Shadows Tribute

    1.   Dark Shadows Tribute (television)
 I. Title

Published by Pioneer Books, Inc., 5715 N. Balsam Rd., Las Vegas, NV, 89130.

First Printing, 1990

—DARK SHADOWS—

Introduction	8
Orgins	10
Dan Curtis	18
Art Wallace	20
Robert Costello	22
What It Is...	24
Jonathan Frid	28
The Reluctant Vampire	34
Barnabas Collins	38
Collinwood Memories	40
Louis Edmonds	44
Grayson Hall	46
Jerry Lacy	48
Alexandra Moltke	50
Star Panel	52
John Sedwick	60
Ron Sprout	62
Appendix: The Episodes	65
A Gallery Of Dark Shadows	133

THE INTRODUCTION

The 1960s was a time of entertainment phenomenons, the likes of which this country has never seen either before or since.

The Beatles arrived in 1964 and changed the face of rock and roll. Two years earlier, Sean Connery had brought Ian Fleming's James Bond to the movie screen in *Dr. No*, beginning a still-thriving series.

In the world of literature, J.R.R. Tolkien's fantasy epic *The Lord of the Rings* and Robert A. Heinlein's *Stranger in a Strange Land* touched the minds of college students, as did the prime time television series *Star Trek*.

Every form of media offered something for the collective cons

cious. Including daytime soap operas. To be more precise, one daytime soap opera.

In 1966, ABC and Dan Curtis Productions introduced **Dark Shadows**, a continuing Gothic romance novel brought to television. The show, which focused on the Collins family, was unexciting and was on the verge of cancellation when Curtis came up with the gimmick which, he hoped, would lure viewers to the program.

Thus was a vampire named Barnabas Collins freed from his sealed coffin to unleash his fury on an unsuspecting Collinsport, Maine. The script, coupled with Canadian actor Jonathan Frid's portrayal of Barnabas, resulted in an overnight sensation. America's newest cult hero was born and **Dark Shadows** became the most widely watched program on daytime TV.

What was originally designed to relieve plummeting ratings became the focal point of the series. As the show developed, audiences were introduced to a variety of supernatural beings which invaded the great mansion of Collinwood, including witches, warlocks, zombies, ghosts and werewolves, populating such themes as time travel, demonic possession and reincarnation.

"The old rule was that you can't give the daytime audience too much at a time because it takes too much of a commitment to watch it every day, and if they have to watch it every day, they won't," Curtis said at the time. "My attitude is that if they have to watch it everyday, we'll get a rating."

He was right. Housewives rearranged their schedules around the show, while children ran home from school in time to watch it. ABC was very much aware of the latter, and as *The New York Times* noted, "moved the show from 3:30 to 4 PM to close the generation gap and allow students to watch the groovy new culture hero do his kinky thing."

The show ran until April of 1971 and spawned two major motion pictures (**House of Dark Shadows** and **Night of Dark Shadows**), a line of best selling paperback books and a soundtrack album. A contingent of fans struck with the same fervor as the Trekkies fueled a merchandising bonanza comparable to the Beatles and *Star Wars*. In

What was originally designed to relieve plummeting ratings became the focal point...

fact, what the Beatles did for moptop wigs, Barnabas did for plastic vampire fangs.

The reason for the success of **Dark Shadows** is difficult to assess. Maybe it was the timing of the show. At its peak of popularity, the Vietnam War was raging in full force and Collinwood was a safe refuge.

Today, some nineteen years after its original run, the show is still enjoying widespread popularity via syndication, video cassette release of the series, fan clubs springing up across the country and conventions held throughout the year in different cities.

The show's continuing popularity surprises many people, including Jonathan Frid.

"I'm amazed that the interest is still there," says Frid. "I thought that two weeks after the show left the air, everybody would forget it."

The Dark Shadows Tribute Book recalls the behind-the-scenes story of America's scariest soap opera. Within these pages you'll learn the various storylines, meet the cast and crew and discover how they brought **Dark Shadows** to the air. You'll explore how fandom has kept Barnabas and the Collins clan alive for all these years. And hopefully you'll have a good time in the land of dark shadows.

—Edward Gross

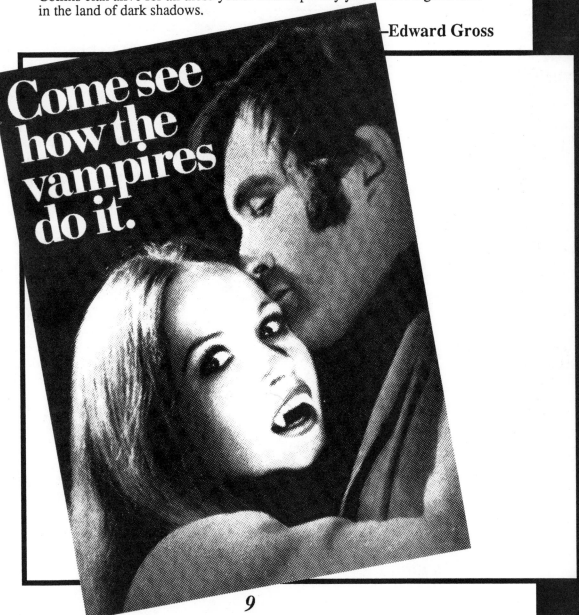

Come see how the vampires do it.

—DARK SHADOWS—

By Edward Gross

The assassination of President Kennedy had delivered the world a numbing blow, but the hysteria which accompanied the arrival of the Beatles a few months later somehow made everything seem alright again. Life in 1964 gave no hint of the turmoil-filled years to come; the world still alive with dreams.

While it's not unusual for a dream to be the basis of goals, it's not common for it to serve as the foundation of a phenomenon which touches the lives of millions. Such was reportedly the case with Dan Curtis and the creation of **Dark Shadows.**

"I awoke suddenly in the middle of a

ORIGINS

strange dream. The bedroom was pitch black, yet I could see the dream clearly," Curtis said in the mid-1960s. "My dream was about a girl riding on a train. She was reading a letter and gazing out the window."

He went on to explain that there was a voice-over which said that she had been hired as a governess at an old place [which would eventually become Collinwood] along the New England seacoast. The dream ended with the girl standing at a deserted station in the middle of the night as the train pulled away.

"I forced myself to come awake and lit a cigarette," he reminisced. "I thought about it and it was brilliantly logical to me."

The next day he told ABC about his dream and they expressed interest in turning the idea into a soap opera. The network gave Curtis a budget and proceeded to turn his dream into reality.

"Yes, that was his famed dream," says Sam Hall, one of the head writers for the series, "but Dan mostly did **Dark Shadows** because he wanted millions of dollars."

As Hall explains it, Curtis had started out selling time for MCA, when, because of his love for the sport, he thought of putting throat mikes on golfers "so you could hear them say 'shit' when they missed.

"He sold that to CBS and it was called *CBS Golf Classics.* He was paid something like $100,000 a week."

The program won an Emmy Award in 1965 and further filled Curtis' streak of independence, causing him to remark that he was "sick of selling other people's garbage."

A man always ready to move on to other things, Curtis got bored with the show and decided that soap operas made the most money, "which they do," Hall says, "and did even more back then because he owned the program."

Curtis' creation was being given life and the executive producer had the enormous task of obtaining a cast and crew. A member of the latter was Art Wallace, who had been a professional singer and and

"I awoke suddenly in the middle of a strange dream...."

was taking voice lessons under the American Theatre wing, when he decided to take a course on writing for television. A script he had written for the course, sold to a television series entitled *The Web*.

"It was live television," explains Wallace. "After that script, they asked me how many I could write in a month. It was a weekly show, a half hour anthological suspense series. After that, I just kept on writing for different shows."

Several years later, Dan Curtis came to him and said that he had a commitment to develop a new daytime show for ABC. He had interested them in doing a Gothic show, although he didn't know what that show would be.

"He wanted to know if I would be interested in producing it," says the writer. "I told him that I wouldn't, but I might be interested in writing and creating it. I had written a one hour movie for *Studio One*, a very prestigious anthology series. My script, called 'The House', was about a woman who hadn't left the house in twenty years, and it was very much like the beginnings of **Dark Shadows**. I used 'The House' as a basis for developing all the characters that were on the show in the beginning. I wrote a bible for the show, and ABC decided to go ahead with it."

It's mentioned that Curtis purports to have created the show from a dream.

"What came to him in a dream, if it was a dream," Wallace questions, "was the idea of doing a Gothic show, but he had no show. He just had the idea of doing a daytime serial which would be different. He had no characters, no story, no nothing. The idea of doing a Gothic show is what interested the network. Now if Dan Curtis dreamed that, then it's fine with me. I wrote the show, creating the actual details. For the first thirteen weeks of the show I wrote the whole thing, 65 scripts.

"In negotiating the contract I had with him," he continues, "he insisted that he wanted to be called the creator of the show, and we went head to head because he didn't create the show, I did. He was totally adamant, so we finally arrived at the conclusion that the credits would read, 'Series Created by Dan Curtis. Story Created and Developed by Art Wallace.' That was just in order to get the contract completed, because he just refused to give up that credit. I would say that his credit should have said, 'Concept by Dan Curtis.' But he wanted that. So I wrote the first thirteen weeks of the show, and after I had done that I found myself getting kind of slap happy. We brought in other writers, and I just kind of supervised."

Curtis next tried to come up with a title for the series. He considered "Terror at Collinwood", "Castle of Darkness" and "The House on Widow's Hill", before finally latching on to **Dark Shadows**.

"The next thing I had to do," Curtis recalled, "was to find a house that could be Collinwood. I sent teams of researchers into the field, but I myself discovered the house we actually used."

Exteriors of the brooding 40 room mansion were shot in Newport, Rhode Island; while footage of Barnabas' Old House was obtained in Tarrytown, New York (where, incidentally, **House of Dark Shadows** was shot); and Essex, Connecticut doubled for the town of Collinsport, Maine.

Hopes were high for the show, but no one—not even Curtis—could have foreseen the phenomenon it would become.

GATHERING THE CREATIVE HANDS

Dan Curtis then began to assemble the crew necessary to bring **Dark Shadows** to the air, starting with a producer. He found one in Robert Costello.

Shortly after World War II, Costello received a Master of Fine Arts degree from Yale University, with the intent of directing theatre. He began work in summer stock and did some instructing, but got sidetracked to Europe where he illustrated a book on theatres, and even designed a theatre. Eventually he came back to the states, still hoping to utilize his degree.

"My problem was I had to support a family, and television had just really started," he explains. "I took a job as a unit manager at NBC, was promoted to associate producer and eventually producer."

In the interim, he did some television directing and got his card from the director's guild. "I planned on entering the entertainment industry," he laughs softly, "little realizing that television would be waiting for me.

"In 1966, I heard a new show was being formed," Costello adds, "and was told that they were looking for a producer, because the guy who created it, Dan Curtis, had only done golf shows. He knew nothing about producing a dramatic show. We met, liked each other and joined with a friend of mine, Art Wallace, who had developed it with Dan and was writing the series."

Two alternating directors were chosen, Lela Swift and John Sedwick, who, like Costello, had a theatrical background, but ended up in television on such shows as *The Nurses* and *Confidential*.

"By the time **Dark Shadows** was getting ready to air, I was, in all modesty, one of the top dramatic a.d.s in television," says Sedwick, "and working on the ABC staff. I joined up with Curtis [because] I just didn't want to do an a.d. job anymore and went out on a limb....thank heavens."

Finally, Robert Cobert was pegged as composer (and his main title theme truly remains one of the eeriest on television) and Sy Tomashoff as scenic designer, a role he excelled at as can be witnessed by the extraordinary sets he created in the studio.

Securing the behind the scenes fixtures, Curtis turned towards casting, claiming that he "wanted somebody with class" to portray Elizabeth Collins Stoddard, the matriarch of Collinwood. He found that somebody in the form of veteran actress Joan Bennett.

"What I really wanted was a play on Broadway," said Bennett, "but it gets very depressing for an actor to just sit around. With my children grown, I was going stir crazy.

"I had never looked at a soap opera in my life," she elaborated, "and I thought they all had rotten actors. I was surprised to find good actors here."

Louis Edmonds, after a career largely made up of theatrical roles, was asked to play Roger Collins, Elizabeth's brother.

"Dan picked me on the way I looked and sounded, which are the two things they go on," explains Edmonds. "Plus an intrinsic quality a person has, whether that be sexual or whatever. I remember I was so pleased because I had a film and was able to tell Mr. Curtis that I was going to Jamaica to shoot this film, and would be happy to call him back. He loved that."

Rounding out the principles were David Henesy as Roger's son, David; Nancy Barrett as Elizabeth's daughter, Carolyn; Alexandra Moltke (now Isles) personifying Curtis' dream as Victoria Winters, the mysterious girl on the train; and Kathryn Leigh Scott as Maggie Evans, a local waitress.

Alexandra Moltke explains that she was contacted by her agent and told that she "was the only innocent looking actress in New York," and that's how she got the part.

Jonathan Frid became the star of DARK SHADOWS

—DARK SHADOWS—

The
DARK
SHADOWS
crew pose
for the
camera

"I had to try several times," Moltke says, "then I had a screen test. Then, oddly, on the screen test I looked like Joan Bennett, which I wasn't supposed to. That added a whole new element to the story, which they resolved later on, that I was supposed to be her illegitimate daughter."

Kathryn Leigh Scott notes that she auditioned for **Dark Shadows** over a period of several months, during which she also did summer stock, rehearsed a play for the O'Neill Festival in Waterford, Connecticut, and had a screen test in Hollywood.

"Those were busy times," she laughs, "but now and again I'd get another call for a reading or camera test. In the end, I had to drop out of the Waterford production to start work on the show.

"I spoke the first lines on that first day of taping," she remembers. "It was also my first time working in front of a live television camera—and I say 'live' because for all practical purposes when the red light flickered on, we taped straight through without stopping no matter what happened. I remember promising God that if I could just get through that day, I'd never act again.

Kathryn Leigh Scott adds, "I just didn't feel suited to the role of Maggie Evans. I liked the role and had given enough good reads and screen tests to be hired, but in those early rehearsals I just couldn't get inside the character. In one of those early days, Bob Costello caught me wondering about my motivation for a particular line. 'How about this,' he said. 'Where're you gonna work tomorrow?' My main memory of those early days had entirely to do with hoping I'd keep my job while I learned to do it."

With cast and crew chosen, **Dark Shadows** began taping during mid-1966 in nearly living black and white (though a transition to color would occur about a year into its run) and differed from other soaps in that it didn't focus on such standard topics as extramarital sex or unwed mothers, but rather on more "Gothic" themes. There were things that went bump in the night, hidden panels and an occasional ghost ("We did two ghost stories before the vampire arrived," Curtis declared).

The first episode was, quite literally, Curtis' dream brought to life. Victoria Winters, a woman with no memory of a personal past, has been hired as governess for young David Collins and is arriving by train. Ms. Winters has accepted the position in the hopes that Collinwood will somehow unlock the mysteries of her past, this despite the objections raised by Roger, who feels that she will merely be in the way and is not needed to supervise his "little monster." Elizabeth insists and has her way.

The intertwining of their lives and the strange happenings which result were among the main elements of the series' first six months.

"It was a Gothic tale about a young governess in a Gothic castle, and surrounded by Gothic people. Very Gothic," Robert Costello laughs. His voice, one notices, carries a certain amount of reverence when talking about the show. "Those early episodes also dealt with what had happened to Elizabeth Collins Stoddard's husband."

Paul Stoddard wanted his wife's fortune and collaborated with one Jason McGuire to steal some legal papers which verified ownership of the vast amount of jewelry and bonds which made up Carolyn Stoddard's inheritance. He tried to leave Collinwood, when Elizabeth found out about his betrayal and struck him across the head with a poker, killing him.

Panicking, she turned to McGuire, who talked her out of turning herself in, hid Paul's body in a trunk and buried it in a room in the basement. This in turn led to his blackmailing Liz. As a result, Elizabeth became a recluse and McGuire periodically reappeared to milk more money out of her.

"They tried to make it look like he had been murdered by accident," says Costello. "Then ghostly sounds began to appear, and a mystery unfolded. The show hobbled along...."

15

"Hobbled" seemed like an accurate word, when one noticed that the ratings were dismal.

"It was sort of a tame mystery," explains John Sedwick, "filled with dark shadows. We had the murder of Paul Stoddard, and later on the ghost of a seaman came back. Actually, in the first few months there wasn't all that much happening."

"The show's basic plotline," Art Wallace interjects, "was very typical of the Gothic novels. The girl comes to the house to be governess to the kid and the house was very mysterious. There was the Heathcliff character, a creep brother and a little boy, and creaky doors. But it wasn't supernatural. It became supernatural during the tenth or eleventh week on the air. I give total credit for that change to Dan Curtis. Dan insisted that it had to become supernatural and not that it 'might be supernatural.' I think he was absolutely right, and that's when our first ghost appeared."

"Our first real ghost story," recalls Costello, "took place when David and a little girl discovered the Old House. They were playing there and were trapped by the evil caretaker, who locked them in a room. Suddenly a little girl ghost appeared to the kids. She was the ghost of a little girl that used to live there. The audience really seemed to like that."

There were several ghost stories, concluding with one in which the caretaker was destroyed by a ghost on Widow's Hill. Then there was a story dealing with Roger's ex-wife, Laura, a phoenix-creature come to claim the soul of her son David.

"When that happened, the ratings began to go up," says Costello. "We tried a few more eccentric things, getting a little bolder and bolder. We found that dealing with the supernatural seemed to increase the audience and there was a better response to the show. We realized that that was the road to follow."

Despite a nudging up in its showing, **Dark Shadows** was still a series threatened to be eclipsed by low ratings.

"The show was limping along, really limping," writer Sam Hall relates, "and ABC said, 'We're cancelling it. Unless you pick up in 26 weeks, you're finished.' Dan had always wanted to do a vampire picture, so he decided to bring a vampire on the series."

"I'd always felt that a vampire was as spooky as we could get," said Curtis. "That if the viewers bought it, we could get away with anything. If it didn't work, I figured we could always drive a stake into his heart."

It worked, and Barnabas Collins was spared the stake.

BRINGING LIFE TO THE UNDEAD

So the decision was made, as a rather desperate attempt to boost the ratings, to add a vampiric element to the show. How does one go about introducing a vampire to the average viewer, and finding an actor capable of making the character a believable one? This was the problem facing Curtis and company, and an original one at that.

They needed an actor who could play a member of the Undead naturally, and yet pass himself off as a human being. Plans called for said thespian to create havoc for a short time, until the ratings went up to a respectable level, and then the vampire would be dispatched.

"At the time," Costello smiles, "we had no idea that the vampire would be the element that saved us, and we were very cautious about approaching it."

As the vampire story drew ever closer, Dan Curtis was in Europe and Costello was left in charge of casting the role.

"We were down to the wire," he says, his voice reverberating with the pressure he felt at the time, "and still looking at actors. As a matter of fact, I had to pose for the portrait of Barnabas which hangs in Collinwood, except for the face, of course. Incidentally, I got the name Barnabas off a tombstone in Flushing. I don't remember the last name, but it was registered in Flushing and dated back to, I think, the 18th Century. The name just sounded right."

During casting calls, an indifferent Canadian actor named Jonathan Frid arrived at the studio. Playing a vampire in a series was the furthest thing from Frid's mind. Getting tied up to a soap opera was contrary to his plans of going to California and becoming an instructor of drama, and he had come to the studio only to placate his agent.

"At the time," Frid recalls, "I said, 'Well, I'm never going to get it, so why am I wasting my time?' I think that because I was in that frame of mind, I ended up getting the job."

According to writer Sam Hall, Dan Curtis had told him that the choice of Frid was made by accident. If so, it was the most fortunate accident that has ever occurred.

"While Dan was in Europe," explains Hall, "he received three photos of the actors the choice had been narrowed down to. Dan was simply to say which one of the three men he wanted to play Barnabas. He sent the pictures back and when he arrived two months later [it was the first day the vampire story was taping], it turned out that they had hired the wrong man. Jonathan Frid was *not* his choice."

John Sedwick differs with this version of the story, "We felt Jonathan played it very honestly. He had a wonderful, mysterious sort of quality...a larger than life quality. He could be an English gentleman on one hand, and on the other he could look evil and exude this vampire-undead mystique."

"When Jonathan Frid appeared," Costello picks up with finality, "We said, 'That's it.' He couldn't have been costumed any faster. A couple of days later, he was in the coffin."

The rest, cliches be damned, was history.

Jonathan Frid, who played Barnabas Collins, is greeted by his thronging fans.

DAN CURTIS

By Edward Gross

Today producer-director Dan Curtis is known for his epic pair of World War II miniseries, *Winds of War* and *War and Remembrance* What seems to have been forgotten is that he was also responsible for some of the finest moments of terror that have graced the television screen.

Curtis was the creative force behind such movies for television as *The Night Stalker*, *The Night Strangler*, *The Strange Case of Dr. Jekyll and Mr. Hyde*, the Jack Palance version of *Dracula* and *Frankenstein: The True Story*. In addition, there was his little horror soap opera named **Dark Shadows**. He created it along with the two feature films it inspired, which he directed. The series became a phenomenon which continues to this day. According to Curtis, the whole thing arose from a dream he had one night in the mid-1960s.

"I awoke suddenly in the middle of a strange dream," Curtis explained. "The bedroom was pitch black, yet I could see the dream clearly. My dream was about a girl riding on a train. She was reading a letter and gazing out the window. There was a voice-over which said that she had been hired as a governess at this old place along the New England seacoast, and it ended with her standing at a deserted station in the middle of the night as the train pulled away and left her there alone.

"I forced myself to come wide awake," he added, "and I lit a cigarette and I thought about it and it was brilliantly logical to me. In the morning I told my wife about it and she thought it was a great idea. She has good taste.

"It just so happens that I had a meeting at ABC that day to discuss another show, but when I told them about my dream, they said, 'Let's do that instead.'"

The result was **Dark Shadows**, a Gothic soap opera in which Alexandra Moltke portrayed one Victoria Winters, new governess at the great mansion of Collinwood, whose life became intertwined with the Collins family as they confronted the usual staples of soap opera life, as well as the occasional ghost and ancient Phoenix.

"I had a meeting with the writers and I said, 'We're going to pull all the stops and have a lot of things happening all the time," related Curtis with a laugh. "The old rule was that you can't give the daytime audience too much at a time because it takes too much of a commitment to watch it every day and if they have to watch it every day they won't. I said, 'If they have to watch it every day, we'll get a rating.'"

Unfortunately, despite Curtis' claims to the contrary, not a great deal happened on **Dark Shadows** during the first six months after its June 1966 premiere.

"The show was limping along, really limping," says writer Sam Hall, "and ABC said, 'We're cancelling it. Unless you pick up in 26 weeks, you're finished.' Dan had always wanted to do a vampire picture, so he decided to bring a vampire on the series."

"I'd always felt that a vampire was as spooky as we could get," admitted Curtis, "that if the viewers bought it, we could get away with anything. If it didn't work, I figured we could always drive a stake through his heart."

The experiment was a great success and the vampire character, Barnabas Collins, struck a...uh...vein with the audience, easily securing a regular position for actor Jonathan Frid on the show, and soon thereafter creating a meteoric rise in the soap's ratings. **Dark Shadows** suddenly found itself in the position of becoming a phenomenon, and creating a movement which continues to this day.

Dan Curtis, a man known for his penchant to get easily bored, constantly strived to add new elements to the series in an attempt to "out-horror" anything the show had done before. The result was oftentimes a confusion that ultimately cost viewers, viewers who began to tune out in droves by the time it went off the air in 1971. In an effort to keep his interest going, he decided to direct several episodes and then get MGM to finance a feature length version entitled **House of Dark Shadows**.

"Dan decided that he was a brilliant director," states Sam Hall, "and he conned MGM into giving him a million dollars for a movie, with him directing. It was his chutzpa, his drive and bullheadedness that enabled him to do it. And of course since then he's done marvelously for himself, what with *The Winds of War* and all."

Curtis followed with a sequel of sorts, **Night of Dark Shadows**, as well as *Burnt Offerings* and the aforementioned Movies of the Week. But since that time, he has moved beyond the genre and, in some ways, seems reluctant to acknowledge ever having been a part of it. He refuses to discuss **Dark Shadows** and has adamantly refused to allow others to pick up the mantle in order to put together a TV reunion film. One almost gains the impression that he is embarrassed of this creation which has taken on a life of its own.

Like Rod Serling's *The Twilight Zone* and Gene Roddenberry's *Star Trek*, Curtis' **Dark Shadows** is a television series that has transcended time, touching new generations as it goes on, inviting viewers into a realm of imagination unlike any other. It's the kind of accomplishment that any creator should be proud of. One can only hope that Dan Curtis will someday come to terms with his creation.

Jonathan Frid, Robert Costello, Dan Curtis and an unknown friend.

By Edward Gross

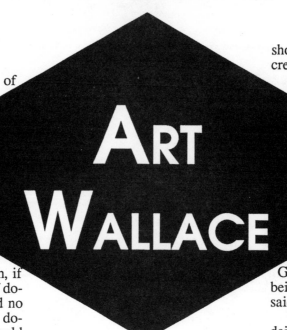

ART WALLACE

Dan Curtis' attribution of **Dark Shadows** to a dream is well known within fandom and the general press, but it's a statement writer Art Wallace doesn't take kindly to.

"It wasn't created by him," exclaims Wallace. "What came to him in a dream, if it was a dream, was the idea of doing a Gothic show. But he had no show. He just had the idea of doing a daytime serial which would be different. He had no characters, no story, no nothing. Now if Dan Curtis dreamed that, then it's fine with me. *I* wrote the show, creating the actual details. For the first thirteen weeks of the show, I wrote the whole thing, sixty-five scripts. In negotiating the contract I had with Dan Curtis, he insisted that he wanted to be called the creator of the show, and he and I went head-to-head on that because he didn't create the show, I did. He was totally adamant, so we finally arrived at the conclusion that the credits would read, 'Series Created by Dan Curtis, Story Created and Developed by Art Wallace.' I think that's the way the credits have read all the time. That was just to get the contract completed, because he just refused to give up that credit. I would say that his credit should have said, 'Concept by Dan Curtis,' but he wanted that. So I wrote the first thirteen weeks of the show, and after I had done that I found myself getting slap-happy. We brought in other writers and I just kind of supervised."

Wallace, whose writing credits range from live television during television's Golden Age to such episodic series as *Star Trek*, based his initial concept of **Dark Shadows** on a script he had written for an anthology series called *Studio One*.

"Dan Curtis came to me and said that he had a commitment to develop a new daytime show for ABC," he explains. "He had interested them in doing a Gothic show, although he didn't know what the show would be. He wanted to know if I would be interested in producing it. I told him that I wouldn't be interested in that, but I might be interested in writing and creating it. I had written a one hour movie for *Studio One*, a very prestigious anthology series. My script was about the woman who hadn't left the house in twenty years, and it was very much like the beginning of **Dark Shadows**.

"The basic plotline," Wallace continues, "was very typical of the Gothic novels. The girl comes to the house to be the governess of the kid and the house was very mysterious. There was a Heathcliff character, a creepy brother, a little boy and creaky doors. But it wasn't supernatural. It became supernatural during the tenth or eleventh week on the air. I give total credit to that change to Dan Curtis. Dan insisted that it had to become supernatural and not be that it 'might be supernatural.' I think he was absolutely right, and that's when we had our first ghost. After the first ghost, the vampire idea came up. It was after Barnabas was introduced that I began to have less and less to do with the

show. Then I just maintained my credit and my royalty.

"But I was there at the beginning of Jonathan Frid. I created Barnabas. It was just about near the end of the first thirteen weeks and we began to talk about where to go next, and by then the show had changed from being Gothic/mystery/melodrama to being supernatural, which, as I said, it wasn't in the beginning."

Wallace, growing tired of the daily grind of doing the show, decided to pursue other interests, but he quickly admits that he thinks the idea of adding a vampire to the mix was a very wise one.

"You're talking to me about it twenty years later," he laughs. "Obviously it was a very wise idea, especially for the time of day it was on. That was when it could get most of the high school kids. It had a very large following. For housewives, I don't think it would have been that wise an idea, but for kids it became a cult thing. The other side of the coin was that as far as daytime serials were concerned, it was not a smashing success. A smashing success lasts fifteen to twenty five years in daytime serial terms. I think the problem is that there was no suspension of disbelief. There was no attempt to say that this is really happening, like *Rosemary's Baby* did. And therefore, after a while it begins to wear out its welcome. After all, how many times can you keep the door creaking? So it was extremely successful, like a Roman Candle, but it fizzled out after five years."

He finds it impossible to gauge how successful the show was in terms of the sheer number of people who watched the series every day.

"I don't know the answer to that," Wallace admits. "That's something you'd have to ask the salespeople. I doubt it sold as

much product as *One Life to Live* or *All My Children* did. I don't know how big the buying audience was in all those kids who ran home from school to watch it. I never did check on what the ratings were. I do know I've been approached ever since to create another show like it. I've created a number of such shows, one of which has been optioned by every network, and optioned several times. But they've never actually gone through with it; dared to put one on. When the final choice was made, they've gone with the normal soap. In that case, **Dark Shadows** was an aberration. As a matter of fact, only the day before yesterday I was talking to the head of programming for CBS and he

felt the time had come for another **Dark Shadows**. But they always say that and never do it."

Wallace sincerely believes a show like **Dark Shadows** could work today, but only if its approach was straighter.

"I think it could work the way *Rosemary's Baby* worked," he points out, "if it were done on a reality basis. **Dark Shadows** became camp and that's why it was so successful, but camp wears itself out. They literally ripped off every horror story. I'm not criticizing it, because that's the way it's done. Just put a new twist on an old story."

Although approached on the subject many times, he is still un-

able to come up with an explanation for the show's ongoing popularity.

"Who can explain a cult?" Wallace asks rhetorically. "I've been involved in two cult projects, **Dark Shadows** and *Star Trek*. They're not the things I'm proudest of doing, but maybe I should be."

By Edward Gross

ROBERT COSTELLO

Once Dan Curtis and Art Wallace established the premise of **Dark Shadows**, the task of finding a creative crew began. One of the first people hired was Robert Costello, who would serve through most of the show's run as producer.

Following World War II, Costello had received a Master's Degree in Fine Arts from the Yale School of Drama. His intention had been to go into directing as he had worked in summer stock and taught intending to work his way into professional theatre.

"I had a family to support," he explains, "and television had just really started. I got an appointment and a job as a unit manager at NBC, then moved to Associate Producer and then to Producer. In the meantime, I did some directing and got my card from the Director's Guild. I didn't fall into it. I planned on entering the entertainment industry, little realizing that television would be waiting for me."

Also waiting for him, although he didn't know it, would be **Dark Shadows** and its cult following.

"I was told that a new show was being formed," Costello recalls, "and they were looking for a producer, because the guy who created it, Dan Curtis, had only done golf shows. He knew nothing about producing a dramatic show. We met, liked each other and a friend of mine, Art Wallace, was involved, so I joined, assembled a crew and we got going. We went on the air in June of 1966 and at that point it was not a vampire show. It was a Gothic tale about a young governess. That's how it started. A Gothic tale with a Gothic castle and Gothic people living in it.

"The pre-Barnabas days," he elaborates, "dealt with what had happened to Elizabeth Collins' husband. We tried to make it look like he had been murdered by accident. He was buried in the basement and then ghostly sounds began to appear. Then a mystery was to be unfolded. It hobbled along and did alright. It was a marvelous looking show. We had Sy Tomashoff as the set designer, and he really did a first rate job. We worked together and I later storyboarded a lot of special effects. We copied them and gave them out to the crew."

Supernatural elements entered the show when the children were trapped in the Old House by the evil caretaker. The ghost of a young girl appeared before them to provide consolation, and the audience immediately took to the idea.

"She was the ghost of the little girl that used to live there," Costello smiles, "and later she became the daughter of two other ghosts that lived in the attic. Then the caretaker was going to do harm to David Collins and his playmate when the portrait of Josette came to life. She was the first real ghost. She glided down from the portrait and saved the children. Then there was the ghost on the hill near the cemetery that came down and destroyed the caretaker.

"When that happened, the ratings began to go up and the audience loved it. We tried a few more eccentric things, getting a little bolder each time. By that time, we had done the ghosts and the horrible death of the guy on Widow's Hill. We found that dealing with the supernatural seemed to increase the audience; we got a better response to the show. We realized that this was the road to follow. We *didn't* realize that the vampire would save us while we were doing it. We were very cautious. I remember Dan was in Europe at the time and the vampire story was coming, so it was up to me to find a vampire.

"We were down to the wire on the story. As a matter of fact, I posed for the portrait, except for the face. The name Barnabas, actually, I got off the tombstone of a graveyard in Flushing. I don't remember the last name, but it was registered in Flushing and dated back, I think, to the 18th Century. That's how we named the character Barnabas Collins. Then Jonathan Frid appeared and we said, 'That's it!' He couldn't have been costumed any faster. He arrived one day and a couple of days later he was in the box."

Although the show has gotten a lot of recognition for its camp appeal, Costello points out rather strongly, no one involved with the series ever laughed *at* the show.

"We enjoyed it," he details, "and we were deadly serious about doing it. It was a very good company. We were doing something that had never been done before, and we were welded together by the oddness of the show. Anyhow, that was the way Barnabas was born, but we were a little tentative about vampires. Where was he going to bite Willie? The first bite Barnabas gave Willie was on the wrist. That's why Jason said, 'Why is your wrist wrapped up like that, Willie?' Then we had him biting sheep and cows. He

had to have something to eat besides Willie. Pretty soon he'd bite anything that moved. The audience didn't seem to mind, so he bit Maggie and he was launched. We even had a sign on the stairway that said, 'Don't forget your fangs.'

"The show was live on tape, but basically live. Editing wasn't very sophisticated back then. There was very little editing done. All the fire effects were created the way you saw them, very quickly."

While Costello calls his four year stint on **Dark Shadows** the greatest "adventure" of his life ("I left the show simply because I was tired!"), he's still at a loss to explain the show's impact, and why it remains so popular.

"It's hard to say," he laughs. "Nobody's ever tried a show like it. I think it proved that there's an audience out there. Nobody likes to do a show that could be terminated. Although it was on the air for five years, they put a soap on with the idea that it will run forever. It just occurred to me that the audience, though it was big, wasn't the one they wanted. They weren't reaching the buying audience. They went up to about age 26 or

so, so advertisers lost thirty percent of the buying audience.

"The show's rating began to eventually slip because Dan (Curtis) lost interest. ABC felt they weren't getting the audience they wanted; they would have to do something with the story because Dan pushed it so fast. He got anxiety attacks, thinking, 'Oh God, nothing's happening today.' It wasn't necessary to rush through the stories. I don't know why he got so nervous. They could have gotten a year or more out of it if they knocked off Dr. Hoffman, who was the only person who knew Barnabas was a vampire. They could have started the cycle all over again.

"Insofar as continuing popularity, it's like the Lucy programs. It was unique in its time. Also, the show could be whatever you wanted it to be. If you wanted it to be high camp, it could be. If you wanted it to be thrillingly real, you could make it that way. It could just be fun. It was anything you wanted it to be, which you cannot say about other shows. They tell you what you must think. **Dark Shadows** could be a variety of things."

By James Van Hise

—DARK SHADOWS—

WHAT IT IS...

Twenty four years after it began, **Dark Shadows** still runs into the same problems of labeling and identification it encountered in the Sixties.

The series began as a soap opera, one of many in the afternoon lineup, but once Barnabas Collins was introduced, things began to change. These changes transformed it from a soap opera to melodrama. Unfortunately, this distinction is often too subtle for modern station managers and programmers. Thus **Dark Shadows** is often picked up for syndication and scheduled either in the morning or at noon since that is, after all, when people watch "daytime dramas." But anyone with the time and energy to do their job properly would read the program guide for the show, watch several episodes and see that vampirism, witchcraft and related story elements push it completely outside the realm of the audience who watches *Days of Our Lives* and *General Hospital*.

Dark Shadows is a mystery/horror/adventure serial with a dark slant. Not the kind of thing viewers of morning and afternoon TV are looking for.

And Barnabas doesn't offer anything that morning TV viewers tune in for. He looks nothing like Phil Donahue and is much too grim to pass as a game show host. In these early slots the series fails to draw an audience. In the early Eighties, two San Diego stations gave the series a try, for example. The first one ran it at 9 AM and when it fared dismally against Phil Donahue, it was canned after three months. Almost four years later a second station picked it up and actually carried it for a year in a noon timeslot before dropping it in favor of a brand new game show. On both occasions, the stations were running the show in the wrong timeslot.

Dark Shadows is not about the infighting or incestuous goings-on of the Collins family. It's a horror show! Its stories get increasingly darker as time goes on. It is clearly better suited for an evening timeslot. A station in Anaheim, California which carries many old TV shows runs the series at 7 PM each week night. It seems to be the perfect period for it. They've figured out what the show really is and have ignored its origins in the late afternoons of the Sixties.

It's not hard to understand why this mistaken impression continues as the early storylines of the series involved Elizabeth thinking she had killed her husband while an old friend of his attempts to blackmail her. Even after Barnabas arrived, it took a few weeks to dispense with a stupid subplot in which the rebellious Carolyn was hanging around with a gang of juvenile delinquents. These familiar and forgettable tales (which are not even offered as part of the syndication package today—although they may possibly be released on video) soon went by the wayside. Willie, who had been the disreputable henchman of Jason McGuire, had the tables turned when

Jonathan Frid, Barnabas Collins, in the chamber of tombs.

his snooping freed Barnabas from his 175 year tomb and Willie found himself under the thrall of this thing from beyond the grave.

Only people who have never watched **Dark Shadows** can call it a "soap opera as the only hand-wringing done on the show is by Barnabas pondering his next blood feast. A contributor to the magazine *Fangoria* once dismissed the show with contempt by saying, "I don't have anything to do with soap operas." In so doing, he displayed his profound ignorance of this important contribution to the horror genre, as **Dark Shadows** outstripped the confines of the soap opera early in its existence and explored as wild and varied an array of story elements as could be imagined.

Beginning with the obvious, there is Barnabas Collins. Traditionally, vampires have been the villain and this is how Barnabas was introduced. He kidnapped Maggie Evans early in his "life" on the show and then turned his attention to Victoria Winters. But every vampire has an origin and so Barnabas was given one and in so doing the character was humanized. We learned what the real Barnabas Collins had been like and how he had been victimized by the witch Angelique and the tragedies that had plagued him because of her. When he returned from the dead as a vampire, Barnabas became bitter and vengeful. He didn't want to be this way, but he had to make the best of it. Now possessed of inhuman powers he used his new-found strength to exact revenge on people whom he felt had done great wrong. The Reverend Trask had persecuted Victoria Winters and so Barnabas shackled Trask inside the wall of the cellar of the Old House and then bricked him in, resulting in his death by suffocation. Even his superstitious, mean-spirited aunt fell when confronted with his inhuman existence and died of fright.

This is not your ordinary vampire or your ordinary vampire story. Usually such stories deal with the pursuit of blood and and the attempts of said vampire to hide from those who would destroy them. The stories of Barnabas dealt with his pursuit of normalcy; his blood thirst but a side angle, although one which dubbed him the mysterious Collinsport Strangler.

Even during the early storylines when the character secretly plotted and carried out his schemes, a glimmer of humanity appeared. This was in the form of the ghost of his long dead nine year old sister, Sara. He'd loved her and mourned her death, and when the ghost of the child refused to appear to Barnabas because of the horrible things he'd been doing, he was deeply hurt. He did have feelings, and it was this that changed him.

Vampire films offer the master of the undead reveling in his existence and enjoying the power it gives over others. Barnabas is a man obsessed with ridding himself of his curse. As time wore on, he displayed increasing anguish every time he had to kill in order to fulfill his bloodthirst. This is not the stuff that average vampire stories are made of.

Dark Shadows may have begun as a typical soap opera

of its day, but it rose above those origins to explore the most bizarre storylines ever to grace television. Its long, successful 1795 flashback sequence, in which all of the actors played the ancestors of their modern characters, led to further and more complicated experiments. These involved meeting alternate versions of the modern characters, including an Angelique who was not evil! The adventures were called "Parallel Time" and involved a foray into a dimension featuring the modern day versions of the characters as well as encounters with 1841 Parallel Time and 1680 Parallel Time, with each getting wilder than the last. There were also excursions into the normal timeline in 1692, 1840, 1897, 1949 and even 1995. Obviously time travel was popular on **Dark Shadows**. In fact, the supernatural was utilized to engage in time travel. When Victoria Winters went back to 1795, it happened during a seance at Collinwood. While Vicki was back in time for months, she only seemed to be gone a moment at modern Collinwood, as she vanished only to be replaced by a stranger who just as quickly vanished when Vicki returned. This is a thoughtful treatment of time travel, showing that a person can spend a week in the past and remain in the present as well. The writers of **Dark Shadows** knew what fruitful territory time travel stories could be as they wrung as many changes on the theme as they could imagine.

Dark Shadows is not a gentle treatment of the fantastic, as stories exploded into violence that shocked television audiences of the day. For instance, the series had never been carried by the network affiliate in Buffalo, New York until 1969 when they began in mid-story. The story involved werewolves, and on the first day it aired, there was a brutal and bloody attack. The show, which aired at four in the afternoon, was met with shock and outrage by viewers accustomed to gentle soap opera fare. They deluged the station with complaints. Buffalo stopped airing **Dark Shadows** after only two days, and the station never publicly acknowledged the negative response they received.

Violence was not that common on **Dark Shadows**, with perhaps one incident a month at best, but compared to other daytime dramas, it was rampant. The outrage which pushed the show off the air in Buffalo apparently arose from a combination of soap opera fans who had no idea what they were getting into and mothers complaining about violence being aired at a time of day when children were watching.

Only people who have never watched the series can refer to it as a soap opera. The sole factor linking it to that style of programming is that it was shot live on tape. All soap operas are shot on videotape, but then so are prime time TV shows. Seeing **Dark Shadows** for the first time, one is immediately struck by the flat look of videotape. A cinematographer I spoke with once remarked that the only thing he thought video was good for was sporting events. It certainly doesn't enhance what is being shot. But in the case of **Dark Shadows**, it actually works in the show's favor. The dark, haunted storylines are bolstered by claustrophobia induced by the flat, indoor lighting which permeates every set, even those which are supposed to be outdoors. No place in Collinsport was bright and cheery. It was as though the town was eternally overcast and on the edge of a violent New England squall. This was perfect for a horror series. When a vampire stalks or a mutilated ghost appears, grim, flat lighting works perfectly to underscore the mood. It also helps cover up the wires of the shoddy vampire bat effect. This was a show about the increasingly monstrous dark sides of these people's lives; people who went through hell to wind up back where they began. While they'd ultimately be no worse off than they were before, they'd be no better off either. They'd just be on hand for the next monstrous interlude in their lives.

It recalls the old Chinese curse, "May you have an interesting life," suggesting that hardship is never dull. On **Dark Shadows**, even the simplest soul led an interesting life.

Perhaps now that **Dark Shadows** is emerging in more syndicated markets and coming out on video cassette, it will garner respect outside the knowing conclave of fans. For they already know the special joys to be found in this romp through the horror of dark shadows.

By Edward Gross

JONATHAN FRID

It was Andy Warhol who said that someday everyone will be famous for fifteen minutes. While this may be an exaggeration of sorts, it is true that the public occasionally latches onto an individual, raising him or her to a fad level or, in some cases, to cult status.

In such situations, said cult objects touch a chord within the public in an inexplicable way and, in a whirlwind of hysteria, become a phenomenon without even realizing it. They just wake up one morning within its midst. Such was precisely the case with actor Jonathan Frid and his portrayal of Barnabas Collins on **Dark Shadows**.

"The success of that show and my character still surprises me to this day," says Frid from his New York apartment.

Several things should be said about Jonathan Frid at the outset, primary among them being that he is not as one would expect.

Knowing him primarily as Barnabas, it's almost, but not quite, disappointing to have him greet you at the door without a flowing black cape draped over his shoulders, candles in hand and fangs protruding from his mouth.

His voice is gentler than one would expect from the world's second most renowned vampire, and while he is a bit grayer than he was on the series, his facial features remain virtually the same. His eyes, in particular, have the same vibrant quality they did twenty years ago.

His apartment, as well, is not as one would expect. Rather than being a shrine to **Dark Shadows**, it is pleasantly decorated, one wall devoted to a career which encompasses everything from Shakespeare to T.S. Elliot to Barnabas Collins.

Jonathan is jovial and an easy talker. Yet as he speaks, one detects a certain amount of self-censorship, a protective device to shield his privacy; a privacy unexpectedly swept out from beneath him in 1967.

"You must realize that being a star is as difficult an art as acting," he says earnestly. "You have to have the right people around you and you have to tell the right lies. You have to be Mr. Perfect from the moment you get up until the time you go to bed. I had a difficult time coping with all that...of dealing with this sudden lack of a private life."

This seems an ironic statement from an actor who strived much of his life for a success like the one he suddenly found himself in.

The beginnings of his attraction to the acting world can probably be traced to his childhood in Hamilton, Ontario, where, while in prep school, the fifteen year old Frid made his stage debut as "old" Sir Anthony Absolute in Sheridan's *The Rivals*.

"Of course the most important role in my life was the first one," he says. "It was during *The Rivals* that I thought, 'Yes, acting is what I can do.' However, it wasn't until five years later, in 1945, while in the navy that it occurred to me to become a professional."

The actor explains that when a navy friend announced that he was "definitely" coming to New York after the war to become a professional, it gave him the same incentive.

Upon leaving the Canadian Navy, he went to England to study at the Royal Academy, which he quit after several terms because, "I wanted to get out and work. I found that many Canadian actors were making a lot of money playing Americans—and I'd gone to the Royal Academy for classical training."

He appeared in a film success called *The Third Man*, portraying an American gangster; and returned to Canada in 1950 to play Dr. Sloper in *The Heiress*. Following this role, Frid studied at Toronto's Academy of Radio Arts under Lorne Green, and then enrolled at Yale Drama School, where, in 1957, he received a Master's Degree in Fine Arts.

Frid moved to New York in 1957 and appeared in *The Golem*, Wallace Hamilton's *The Burning*, *Romeo and Juliet*, *Macbeth* and *Richard III*, among others. Despite all this, success still seemed intangible, though, perhaps, barely visible.

It was in the beginning of 1967 that fate intervened and altered Frid's life in ways he could not foresee.

He had just wrapped up a national tour with Ray Milland in *Hostile Witness*, and his plans were to pack up his belongings from his apartment, move to California and utilize his Master's Degree to get a job as a professor of drama.

"As I got to my apartment door in New York, the phone was ringing," he recalls. "I left my bags in the hall and ran in to answer it. It was my agent, who I hadn't told when I'd be back. He told me about the part of a vampire on **Dark Shadows**, and coaxed me

into trying out for it by pointing out that the job would only last a few weeks and would net me some extra money to go to the coast with. Well, you know the rest of the story. It was just that freaky phone call. If I had been two minutes later...." His voice trails off, letting the silence speak for itself.

Frid joined the series in April of 1967 and the rest, as they say, was history. The ratings took off and fan mail began pouring in, including suggestive letters and nude photos of women who wanted him to use his fangs on them. Vampire Barnabas Collins and Jonathan Frid were suddenly cult objects.

"Barnabas is very much like everything I've played before," Frid explains. "I played Macbeth once, and there's a great similarity between Macbeth and Barnabas. Certainly Macbeth is built on guilt, just as Barnabas was. It's a characteristic which even Richard III has, though I don't really like to drag Richard into it. A lot of people think that he had no guilt, and I think that he did." To illustrate, Frid points out the nightmare sequence of Shakespeare's play in which Richard confronts the souls of his victims, and, consequently, himself.

"I've often portrayed the heavy and it's a type of role I enjoy playing," he continues. "My greatest 'heavy' role, next to Barnabas, was definitely Richard III. It's the one which I would love to play again, though I'm almost getting too old for it." He pauses at this, his eyes taking on a contemplative look.

"Richard III is a delightful role that can be played very comically, but I was playing it for horror."

With this, Frid gives an oration on the aspects of his portrayal which has apparently influenced many of his other roles. "I love to play horror for horror's sake," he explains. "Inner horror...I mean. I never thought I created fear with the fang business of Barnabas. I always felt foolish doing that part of it. The horror part I liked was 'the lie.'

"There's nothing more horrible than looking someone in the eyes who's telling you a lie and you know it. Somehow that scares me more than anything else. Of course I've never been physically attacked by anybody with a knife or a gun...or teeth, and that may be quite horrible. But in terms of the theatre, I liked the inner drama rather than the outward manifestation. An inner conflict or emotional confrontation is more of a drama to me. That's why with Barnabas there were many scenes I was thrilled to do and why the show came alive so many times for me."

It was Barnabas' lie, that he was pretending to be something that he wasn't, which motivated Frid more than any other aspect of the role. "That pretense was something the actor playing Barnabas had to remember all the time," he emphasizes. "He got the lust for blood every once and a while, but always what preyed on his mind was the lie.

"And of course it played right into my lie as an actor," he adds. "I was lying that I was calm and comfortable in the studio, just as Barnabas was lying that he was the calm, comfortable cousin from England. He wasn't at all. He was a sick, unbelievable creep that the world didn't know about."

In essence, the character's facade inspired the actor, but what was it about Barnabas that appealed to so many people?

"First of all," Frid begins, obviously still trying to explain it in his own mind as well, "Barnabas was the first sympathetic vampire. He was a man with an addiction who drank blood only to survive. The audience felt pity for him, and many of the women wanted to mother him. There was a love/hate relationship between the audience—particularly children—and Barnabas. In some ways, he was looked upon as a darker version of Santa Claus; friendly enough that you were intrigued by him, yet mysterious enough that he frightened you."

And what about the overall appeal of **Dark Shadows** itself?

"I recently watched a re-run of an episode which I thought was excellent, and it gave me a perspective which is good for me to have. It took me out of my own ego trip in my connection to the show, because I wasn't even on it, and I think it answers that particular question.

"Grayson Hall as Dr. Hoffman and Robert Gerringer as Dr. Woodard were having an awful confrontation about me," Frid says. "This day, they were both dead-on perfect and their confrontation sparked. It reinforced our interest in her getting her goals. Grayson was strong without overacting and made everything believable in this ridiculous story. But that's the magic of theatre, making implausible things plausible. The writers scored that day as did the actors, and it was all very believable."

He continues, obviously enthused by this revelation. "A great deal of the time the show was absolutely absurd, because we weren't strong enough to make it believable and we had an extra duty over and beyond the average soap opera. To deal with this strange material on a daily basis is more demanding on the actors than normal, and on the writers. Because of its inconsistency as a good and bad show, some days people would laugh at it as a hoot and then on others they would get caught up in it.

"I suppose what I'm really trying to say is that when the oversizeness is honestly thought out and meaningful, the show became sheer magic. It's as good as anything I've ever seen on television."

By the summer of 1967, it had become obvious **Dark Shadows** was a sensation. Teenagers gathered outside the studio to get a glimpse of their favorite star, fan mail had increased ten-fold and, thanks to a *New York Times* article which revealed that Frid had a listed phone number, fans called at all hours of the night. It wasn't long before his likeness adorned lunch boxes, bubble gum cards, comic

31

books and more than a dozen paperback novels. One must assume that being thrust into this phenomenon was not an easy thing to deal with.

"Well, the cameras scared me because I hadn't had much experience in television," Frid admits. "Not so much the cameras, but the millions of dollars they represented. I was in big business and my job was to get people to hang in there until the next set of commercials. I was scared by that.

"The other aspect," he continues, "is the stardom. I guess I kind of realized what was happening after two or three months, but I was saved from dwelling on it and becoming too big for my boots because I was so busy with the scripts every day."

Actually this does not seem so improbable when one understands Frid's approach to studying a script.

"The character of Barnabas was all set before we even began. My only problem was getting it under my belt. Getting the lines down, delivering them and playing the values I had to play; the motivations. I spend so much time working out the problems that I don't get down to the nitty gritty and get the bloody lines learned. I'm constantly undoing whatever it is I'm doing. Tearing it apart so it's in a shambles, little pieces of paper all over the place. Then I have to be in front of the camera in half an hour, and I've got my part all over the place. I used to do this night after night after night. It's just in my nature."

Success followed success, as Frid toured different cities on weekends, hosted pageants, appeared on TV talk shows, starred in the big budget motion picture **House of Dark Shadows** and even visited the White House. But after a five year run, it was over; ratings declined and the show was cancelled in April of 1971.

"The end wasn't really a great shock, because the writing on the wall was always there for me," Frid says. "Every time the show went up another notch, I figured it

was peaking and that it would start to go down. It lasted a hell of a lot longer than I thought it would. It wasn't the average soap opera and they went through all the stories three or four times. We started repeating ourselves and the show burned out."

So, with the exception of the hardcore fans, **Dark Shadows** faded into the mists of time, and the hysteria which had snared Frid, suddenly set him free again.

"I knew I couldn't make a career out of being a star, because I would have had to make a commitment to the occult," he states. "I have no interest in the occult at all. If I did make a career of it, I would have had to become an honorary member of every occult society in the country and get into vampirism. I just couldn't bear the thought of doing that. Look at Bela Lugosi, the poor man. He died and had himself buried in his Dracula cape. I never wanted to get like that."

Moving out of the shadows, Frid appeared live in *Murder at the Cathedral* and on film in Oliver Stone's *Seizure* and ABC's *The Devil's Daughter* before dropping out of the public spotlight. Was the problem typecasting?

"I knew that was going to happen," he explains. "Actually there was nothing to typecast except the fangs. As far as Barnabas was concerned, he was more of a full-blown character than anybody on the show. Frankly, if I had worked harder, I could have manipulated it or, indeed, exploited it. You see, being a star is a big job and you can never go back. You can try, but you always end up trying to top yourself."

Another thing which made Frid keep a low profile was a desire for normalcy. He disassociated himself from continued interest in the show for nearly a decade.

"It was just such a pleasure to have my private life again," he says with a breath of relief. "I was just so bored with the whole **Dark Shadows** thing."

In fact, it wasn't until the early 1980s that Frid first appeared at

his first convention, and his interest has been re-sparked, at least to a degree.

"It's absolutely wonderful that the fans have kept this whole thing alive," he laughs. "And in a way, my re-association with them has allowed me to utilize **Dark Shadows** as a springboard for a live show I've created."

This one man show, which has gone through a variety of titles including *Genesis of Evil* and *Fools and Fiends*, has met with great success as the actor has taken it around the country.

"It's shaping up nicely," he enthuses. "I've had my vacation from show business and now it's time to get back to brass tacks."

The future bodes well, and Jonathan Frid, classical actor and consummate vampire, embraces it willingly.

—DARK SHADOWS—

RELUCTANT VAMPIRE

By James Van Hise

He was a vampire brought in to give new life to the anemic plotlines of a sagging soap opera. His character, originally conceived as being temporary, grew to become the centerpiece in what quickly became the first and only supernatural soap opera. Barnabas Collins was the vampire who rescued **Dark Shadows**.

Shifty servant, Willie Loomis, in search of legendary jewels believed buried with Collins ancestors, stumbled on the secret room of the Collins family mausoleum. There he found a coffin chained shut. Breaking the locks, he at last opened the casket, only to be greeted by a hand reaching out to grab him by the throat. From that day forward, Willie (played by John Karlen, seen most recently on *Cagney and Lacey* and *Snoops*) was the helpless servant of Barnabas.

At first, Barnabas was a master of villainy. Pretending to be a long lost cousin and descendent of the original Barnabas, he showed up at the door of Collinwood claiming to have just arrived from England. Although the Collins family professed ignorance of any living relatives in that country, his uncanny resemblance to the 200 year old portrait of the original Barnabas, now prominently displayed in the foyer of Collinwood, supported his claim. In keeping with their sense of family, Elizabeth Collins allowed Barnabas to live in the long unoccupied Old House on the Collins estate. This suited Barnabas since it had actually been his home two centuries before.

Behind the walls of the Old House, far from the eye and ear of the curious, Barnabas went about his private business. With Willie to protect him by day, Barnabas adopted the guise of a businessman away all day, only calling on relatives and acquaintances at night. His coffin was moved from the mausoleum to the basement of the Old House.

Barnabas was ruthless and more than once committed murder to protect his secret and dispose of adversaries who proved genuinely threatening. He could have lived securely at the Old House despite his occasional forays into Collinsport to attack young women (which earned him the reputation of the mysterious Collinsport Strangler), but he became brazen.

Upon meeting Maggie Evans, he was struck by her resemblance to his long-lost Josette. With Willie's aid, he kidnapped Maggie and hypnotized her into believing she was indeed Josette. This spell finally wore off and she became a tormented woman, held captive in a cell in the basement of the Old House. Barnabas became furious when he couldn't bend her to his will. This was compounded when a strange little girl began appearing to Maggie—the ghost of Barnabas' long lost sister, Sara. Sara finally helped Maggie escape and protected her thereafter.

As Barnabas Collins, Jonathan Frid played a reluctant vampire who didn't enjoy putting the bite on people.

When Maggie was found, she was hysterical, suffering from memory lapse. A doctor whose care she was placed in, one Julia Hoffman, began to piece together clues and finally confronted Barnabas. Dr. Hoffman wasn't out to expose Barnabas, but rather to make him her patient. Since Barnabas secretly hated his vampiric existence, he agreed to Julia's arrangement, but made it clear that should she ever betray him, he'd kill her. He often angrily stressed this point to Julia by grabbing her throat and squeezing just enough to emphasize his displeasure. Julia tolerated this treatment at his hands because she found herself attracted to him, although he scorned her advances.

Julia Hoffman (Grayson Hall) began a series of injections designed to treat Barnabas' condition medically. Although the treatments seemed to be gradually working, Barnabas demanded the process be accelerated. He had become infatuated with Vickie Winters, the governess at Collinwood, but he didn't want to press his attentions unless he could do so without any danger of exposure. Were he normal, that problem would be solved.

His impatience nearly cost him everything when the increased doses caused him to age to the actual physical state of a man two centuries old. While Dr. Hoffman was able to reverse the effect, Barnabas refused to continue her experiments and sent her away. Julia then insinuated herself back into his life and even placed her diary with an attorney so that it would be read in the event of her death. It was the only hold she had over him as her jealousy over his interest in Vickie was ill-disguised.

Then the gradual change in Barnabas began. We learned the secret origin of his vampirism and how he had fallen victim of a witch's curse!

In the year 1795, Josette DuPres arrived from Martinique with her handmaiden, Angelique. Because Angelique secretly loved Barnabas, she bewitched both Josette and Barnabas' cousin so that the two would become lovers and secretly marry before anyone could stop them. Heartbroken, Barnabas challenged his cousin to a duel and killed him. Barnabas retreated to an enforced solitude in the Old House where he and Josette were to have lived when they married. There, Angelique tricked Barnabas into agreeing to marry her, should she cure the seemingly fatal illness of his young sister, Sara. After they married, Barnabas discovered the truth about Angelique. She was a witch who caused Sara's torment in order to force the marriage and the one behind other recent calamities that had befallen the Collins family. When Barnabas confronted her and vowed his hatred, Angelique began to wreck vengeful destruction on the Collins clan, including the death of Sara. Finally, Barnabas confronted Angelique and shot her.

Believing herself dying, she cursed Barnabas and he was attacked by a bat. Barnabas fell unconscious and died. Angelique recovered and realized what she had done and what would happen to Barnabas. The night he was buried she went to his tomb to prevent his return from the dead into a cursed life. Instead Barnabas gained his revenge on Angelique, killing her in the mausoleum.

Using her faithful servant, Ben Stokes (Thayer David), Barnabas led a secret existence until discovered by his father. Then his mother, Naomi, learned the truth, the final shock for her, she took her own life. Attempts to cure Barnabas failed, so his father tried to shoot him, to no effect. Finally, during the day, his father had Barnabas chained in his coffin and placed in the secret room of the Collins family crypt.

In modern times, when Barnabas lost faith in Dr. Hoffman, he found another doctor to gave him hope. Following an auto accident, Barnabas awoke in a hospital. There, one Dr. Lang showed him how long he had been unconscious by pulling aside a curtain to reveal that it was mid-day. Barnabas screamed in horror, but found that he was unharmed. The doctor had analyzed the peculiar blood of Barnabas and treated him with a serum which temporarily provided a cure. Whenever the vampire would feel his old urges calling him to seek out lifeblood, Dr. Lang would give him another injection.

Angelique would not be denied vengeance, however. She returned from the spirit realm to bedevil Barnabas again and undo his chance for a normal life. Dr. Lang had come up with a method to create a human being from the parts of dead bodies. He planned to transfer the lifeforce of Barnabas into this body, ending his curse. Angelique attempted to prevent this by killing Dr. Lang. Julia was able to complete the experiment, but it failed, although it did bring life to the body created by Lang.

Barnabas eventually relapsed into vampirism, but he also became more humane. This began when his heinous deeds were rebuked by the ghost of Sara Collins. She confronted him and said she avoided him because of his evil. Terribly hurt by her words, when she vanished vowing never to see him again unless he changed his ways, Barnabas began to change. We saw the vampire as a man. When his origin was related in detail, it became clear that Barnabas had been a kind, gentle man. When transformed into a vampire, his unearthly thirst and inhuman powers robbed him of his human soul.

Yet there was more to him than that. His struggle with his secret urges and his guilt over what powers beyond his control forced him to do to survive made him much more than the average night stalker in search of a bloody delicacy. It made him a vampire attempting to hold on to his fleeting humanity.

—DARK SHADOWS—

Barnabas Collins was a vampire trapped by his curse.

By Sidney J. Dragon

BARNABAS COLLINS

It was early one Sunday morning about 3 o'clock, when I received a call from my publisher. He was very excited as he told me of my latest assignment —to interview Barnabas Collins.

Two days later, I was packed and heading up to Collinsport, Maine to interview Mr. Collins. I arrived just before dusk on the steps of the Old House. Willie Loomis, who worked for Barnabas Collins, led me into a richly furnished drawing room. He told me to make myself at home and that Mr. Collins would be in shortly. He then shuffled out of the room, mumbling to himself. I began scanning over the books that were on one of the many bookshelves. I noticed Poe, Dickens and Stoker, among other Victorian authors.

The mantle clock was striking 6:30 as Mr. Collins entered the room.

"Good evening, Mr. Dragon, isn't it?"

"Yes. Call me Sidney."

"I am Barnabas Collins. You're from the *Collinsport Record*, aren't you?"

"Yes. I'm supposed to interview you. I'm a bit nervous since I've never met a vampire before."

"No need to be nervous. You can just say that I work what's commonly known as the grave-yard shift."

"You certainly have a good sense of humor about it."

"I have to, to keep my sanity. Shall we sit down and make ourselves comfortable?" he suggested, motioning to a large, overstuffed, high-backed Victorian chair. I sat down and so did he.

This was when I began the interview.

"What was it like being locked in a coffin for 150 years?"

"Dark and lonely," he replied bluntly.

"What were your first thoughts when you were released?"

"Well, as you can imagine, the first thing I asked Willie was, 'What year is this?' Naturally, he thought he was seeing things. I must say 1966 was vastly different from 1795. Back in my time, we didn't have automobiles, telephones...didn't have many things." He smiled and gazed out the window and into the darkness as if reflecting upon it all.

"When you first met Angelique, did you think she would become so obsessed with you?"

"No, and I didn't feel for her what she felt for me. As far as I was concerned, she was there for one reason and one reason only. She should have known her place in life, which was to serve the upper class. At the time, I didn't have Josette and she was available. However, she should have known better than to form any kind of attachment for me."

I felt enough had been said about her, so I decided to change the subject.

"In contrast, which time would you prefer to live in—the present or the time you were born in to?"

He considered the question a bit and slowly answered. "Well, the 1700's were much simpler, but with everything that happened back then, I'd say the present."

"When did you begin to think of Willie Loomis more as a friend than a servant?"

Barnabas smiled as he said, "After we grew to respect and trust one another. I must say he took some getting used to, and I'm sure he felt the same way about me. It's not every day that one becomes employed by a vampire." He chuckled a bit and said, "It was probably when he helped me fight Angelique with the dream curse that our relationship became more than just master and servant. We became friends."

"Do you ever think you'll be cured of your vampirism?" I asked. "And if so, how could that come about?"

"No." He paused before going on. "I don't think I will ever really be cured of Angelique's curse. I'd have to return to the past and destroy her before she made me what I am now. However, if I did that, you would not be sitting here now interviewing me."

"Regarding 1795, what memories stand out clearer than the others?"

"The deaths of Sara and Josette, my causing those deaths and my own death before I became one of the Undead."

"How has being a vampire changed you?"

"Being alone in my coffin and knowing that no one can truly share or understand my existence."

"What do you do to pass the time outside of your coffin other than your nocturnal wanderings and needs?" I hoped I was wording it delicately enough.

"Talking to Julia about history. As you may know, I'm quite interested in the history of what transpired in Collinsport while I was inside my coffin."

"This next question may sound strange, but is being 'Undead' all it's cracked up to be?"

"What do you mean?"

"Well, people sometimes say thing like, 'I'd like to live forever.'"

"No they wouldn't. If they only knew. One of the fundamental things in life is change, and when you're one of the Undead, you yourself don't—can't—change. Losing loved ones is never easy, but living on endlessly while they grow old, fade away and die is the worst kind of pain. So in answer to your question, no, it's not all it's cracked up to be."

I hesitated to ask the next question, but I knew I must. "What were your thoughts the first time you had to drink blood?"

"I was repulsed and still am."

"Why?"

"Because, no normal human being thinks about drinking blood. I was disgusted with myself and I loathed Angelique for making me this way. It was totally sick. I didn't know how I could endure being this way forever."

"When you met Lieutenant Forbes, did you think he would turn out to be such a con man?"

"Of course not. He was seeing Millicent, and we often talked. I would never have been friends with him if I had known what scoundrel he was!"

"It seems you have a proper perspective about everything, including your, well, should I say, 'condition.'"

"I suppose I do. It comes from years of experience, because there are certain things that can destroy you if you take them to heart."

Just then, a knock came at the door. Barnabas Collins rose and said, "If you will excuse me."

"Yes, of course," I responded.

He left the room and I could hear faint voices. Then he brought in a lovely young brunette girl. I couldn't help but think from the way he looked at her that perhaps there was a ray of sunshine in his existence after all.

"Come in here, my dear. There's someone I want you to meet. This is Mr. Dragon. He has been interviewing me for his newspaper. Mr. Dragon, this is Miss Winters."

"Hello, Miss Winters."

"Mr. Dragon, it's nice to see you." She then turned to Barnabas Collins and said, "Elizabeth wants to see you right away at Collinwood. She said it's important. Also, you received a telephone call from a Mr. Clark about buying some property."

"Oh, yes. I did have an appointment with him. You'll have to excuse my eccentricities, Mr. Dragon. I do not have a telephone, and as you can see, I do not have electricity. I never could get used to some things. You will also have to excuse me as I must go to Collinwood. Perhaps we can talk further at some other time."

I thanked him and we said our goodbyes. I registered at the Collinsport Inn for the night. As I ate my dinner, I thought back over *my* interview with a vampire, and I prayed he could find some peace. I slept well, undisturbed by bad dreams, and by five o'clock the following day, I was back in New Orleans in a taxi heading home to my typewriter.

—DARK SHADOWS—

COLLINWOOD MEMORIES

By John Larsen and Joanne Larsen-Verducci

Collinwood. A place of ghosts and ghouls, witches and warlocks, vampires and werewolves. A sprawling, brooding family mansion where the Collins family live out their strange, troubled existences. High on a hill overlooking the sea, Collinwood has seen its share of the supernatural. The vast and rambling estate has long been populated by queer, otherworldly characters, living purely for the pursuit of evil, others merely prisoners of sinister spells that span time itself.

[However] in April of 1967, after ten months on the air, **Dark Shadows** was low in the ratings and in danger of being cancelled until Dan Cur

Collinwood. A place of ghosts and ghouls, witches and warlocks, vampires and werewolves. A sprawling, brooding family mansion where the Collins family live out their strange, troubled existences.

tis devised the perfect "hook" for viewers: a 175 year old vampire! Jonathan Frid was cast as the bloodthirsty Barnabas Collins and from the beginning, he was clearly no ordinary vampire. Frid's chilling portrayal of Barnabas as a vampire who loathed his vampirism shattered all the preconceptions that the public had. The role was all the more thrilling and thought-provoking as a result. While Barnabas' need for blood drove him to destroy, his pangs of conscience evoked the audience's sympathy. The show's ratings skyrocketed and Frid received thousands of letters each week from his loyal fans. "It really got out of hand," he recalls. "I just couldn't read 1500 letters a day. But I enjoyed the mail and still do."

One must understand the rigors of soap opera production to truly appreciate the magic that the cast and crew of **Dark Shadows** created. In one day, the producers were responsible for taping what it would often take weeks to produce on a film set. "It was like jumping off a tall rock into water thousands of feet below," Frid comments. "I had to do it every morning whether I liked it or not, so I really pushed myself. But it was very, very difficult for me."

For the next few years the show remained high in the ratings as it explored plots involving time travel, witchcraft, hangings, beheadings, live burials, ghosts, zombies, werewolves and the like. The ratings would jump with each new skeleton that fell out of the Collins family closet. In 1971, the writers realized that they had run out of skeletons. During the five years that the show had been on the air, every supernatural trick in the book had been used, and despite protests from the legions of fans who watched every afternoon at 4:00, **Dark Shadows** was cancelled on April 2, 1971. Line producer Robert Costello, who had left the series in 1969, believes that the show would have become too cliched and confusing if allowed to continue. "At least we can say that **Dark Shadows** died in pretty good shape," he comments.

The show was made available for syndication through Worldvision Enterprises and repeats began turning up in 1975, but syndication was very limited and only a small portion of the series 1245 episodes were available at that time. Then in 1982 a major effort was launched and the show began playing in many major markets across the country, and has currently found new life in MPI's video release of the episodes (at the time of this writing, the first 80 episodes have been made available).

The continued success of **Dark Shadows** may have more to do with the overwhelming fan interest than the nightly ratings. Through the years, thousands have worked tirelessly in support of the show, encouraging the syndicator to release more episodes and petitioning stations across the country to give the series a try. Many stations have found the show a tremendous success and more and PBS outlets have come to view the series as a powerful asset. These stations rely heavily on financial support from the viewers and are constantly amazed by the loyalty of the fans.

Fandom dates back as far as the show itself and has continued to grow. It would be impossible to list all of the groups now in operation. They keep the fans up to date with syndication and video news, reports on the stars' present activities, publications and the conventions that droves of fans attend each year. Festivals not only reunite the fans, but the stars themselves. Former performers such as Jonathan Frid, Joan Bennett, Marie Wallace, Terry Crawford, Donna Wandry and Sharon Smyth are on hand to discuss the show.

Looking back on **Dark Shadows** after twenty four years, the stars have fond memories and funny stories to share with their fans. Many of the anecdotes revolve around the show's hectic pace, tight schedule and low budget. A typical day at the studio included precious few rehearsals and little room for mistakes once the cameras were rolling. Even though the episodes were taped seven to ten days before airtime, the show was done "live on tape." Since editing the tape after every mistake was far too costly, many of the glaring errors could never be corrected and are still seen today on the reruns. For instance, the dark shadows at Collinwood often included the one cast by a boom microphone careening across the set. Actors flubbed their lines and couldn't go back to try it again. If an actor should happen to knock over a tree while strolling through the "woods" or a tombstone in the "cemetery," he would usually continue on his way as though nothing had happened. Dan Curtis probably cornered the market on insect repellant, but a fly or two would still creep past the cameras on occasion. More often than not the little bugger would ham it up by hanging around for a little while, creating a sticky situation. Jonathan once delivered a chilling speech about how he was going to bump somebody off, while swatting at the fly which had landed on his face and was persistently buzzing around his nose.

Louis Edmonds who played Roger Collins in the present-day sequences as well as several of the Collins ancestor in time travel stories, tells of the day he forgot a scene he was supposed to play at the end of an episode. "I had walked up the stairs to my dressing room, thinking I was done for the day. So I pulled down my britches and was loosening my tie, when Bob Costello flew up the stairs to my dressing room and said, 'You're not through yet!' and I said, 'Hold the tape! Hold the tape!' and just screamed that all the way down the stairs." Other performers in the

same scene with Louis recall him running down the stairs while getting dressed and racing onto the set in his underwear. With no time to get his pants on, Louis was featured in close-up, holding a brandy glass, while the viewers had no idea of what was going on from the waist down. It took every bit of his co-stars' strength to play the scene straight, without cracking up.

In other cases, it was the absurdity of the situation that the characters were in that would crack up the actors. The characters were constantly exposed to ghosts, ghouls and assorted creepies, and the performers would often break into fits of hysterical laughter as soon as the scene ended and the little red light on the camera went off. Sometimes they weren't able to contain themselves that long, as Donny Wandrey, who portrayed Barnabas' love interest, Roxanne Drew, explains.

"We were in the throes of a series of astrological readings one day, David Selby [Quentin Collins], Chris Pennock [Gabriel Collins] and I, and David who has always had a wonderful sense of humor, just lost it, flung himself over the table and threw the cards all over. I thought, 'They're going to stop for this,' and I kept going...so I'm going, 'It seems here you're to be wed in three months,' and he got hysterical. The whole show's on tape. They never cut anything! Chris Pennock finally pulled him together and we went on with the scene. I was sure we'd retape it, but it was really live tape and that meant that you only did it once!"

Occasionally, something terribly drastic would occur and the scene would simply have to be redone. But more often than not, the cameras kept rolling through every crisis. Jonathan Frid's favorite blooper proves that the actors weren't safe even after the actual show had already been taped!

"At the end of the show they would always run the credits over one of the sets that we had used that day, but the set was supposed to be empty," Jonathan explains. "So they used to cordon off that set to make sure nobody crossed it after the show was over. On this day the credits were running over a shot of the hall in the main house and I was unaware that the set had been cordoned off because I came around the back way. So I sashayed right on through the hall carrying my costume, my shoes, socks, ties and underwear! Sure enough, there I was on TV two weeks later! How anybody interpreted that story, I'll never know."

Although the cast of **Dark Shadows** has gone on to other projects, the show still occupies a special place in their hearts.

By Edward Gross

LOUIS EDMONDS

Louis Edmonds was involved with **Dark Shadows** from the first day of taping in 1966 to the last in 1971. He was initially cast as Roger Collins, brother of Collinwood matriarch Elizabeth Collins-Stoddard. When the show flashed back to 1795, the actor portrayed Joshua Collins, father of Barnabas and the man who had chained his vampire son in a coffin, where he would remain for nearly two centuries. Through the show's five years, he portrayed a variety of roles in different time periods, concluding with a butler characterization in a revised version of *Wuthering Heights* (actually a parallel time storyline). Most recently he has achieved super stardom as Langley Wallinsford in *All My Children*.

Since the time of this interview, Edmonds has appeared at several conventions for the show. Bearing this in mind, the odds are that he has become considerably more aware of the phenomenon than evidenced here.

"I am now in a better frame of mind," then when he first worked on a cult show, he admits. "It's as simple as that. Apart from that, I love the job I have. I think anybody who's an actor in New York is lucky. We're really the aristocrats of show business, employed actors. It is, however, demanding work. They have worked out a technique for putting on a show that they didn't have in the days of **Dark Shadows**. They're able to figure out how to cut material we won't use, and therefore save us hours of rehearsal. We used to, for instance, be given a blocking session. That meant a trip all the way across town, and then you'd have to come back the next morning. Little things like that have been worked out. It's good work, although I'm really not too

pleased with the progress I've made in front of the camera. I'm more at ease, to be sure, but I would like to show myself more knowingly with the camera. I'm not intimidated by it, but I don't know how to make love to it, as the expression goes, because there's never time."

When asked how similar his two roles of Roger and Langley were, the actor responds, "I really don't know how to answer that. I would be willing to bet the first thing you would notice is that the quality of my voice sounds older, which is fascinating to me. After the age thing, I would rather expect they were the same. With Langley, I pretend, and the audience pretends, that he was rather poorly born, without any benefits, but with a fire in him for self-improvement. The writers do very nicely by both me and Langley. Like the character of Roger Collins, he's a black sheep, but hopefully he's got some kind of charm that makes him tolerable."

Edmonds became involved with **Dark Shadows** due to the actions of a friend. "Alan Shane," he explains, "was a friend of mine in those days in New York. He was also a casting manager, and he drove me around as a possibility as Roger Collins for Dan Curtis. Dan picked me on the way I looked and sounded, which are the

two things they go on. Plus an intrinsic quality a person has. I remember I was so pleased with myself, because I had a film and was able to tell Mr. Curtis that, 'I am going to Jamaica to shoot a film, and I'd be happy to call you when I get back.' He loved that. I shot the film and started the show."

Adding Barnabas Collins changed **Dark Shadows** completely as the series moved far more firmly into the supernatural. Edmonds explains, "There was more excitement when the Barnabas thing came along. It was the same level of production, though they did go into the extraordinary thing with the vampire and the special effects. In fact, some days the actors would not get time to run through anything, because they would take all the time to get some dazzling effect. We were praying that we'd know the lines before we got out there.

"I do remember that Jonathan came on the set, and it was almost as though we'd known each other for a long time. I don't see him too often anymore, but he's still a very close friend. We had too much bizarre fun when we got into the vampire story.

"Hundreds of children were standing in front of the studio. We knew we had something bigger than life on our hands. I had never been in such an exciting success before in my life."

Dark Shadows was different than any other series on the air, either before or since. And Edmonds feels that was the main appeal of the show. "It's different, I guess. Mind you, I'm thinking of these things for the first time. I've never given much thought about dear old **Dark Shadows**. The ghoulish quality appealed to young children. Joan Bennett and Nancy Barrett and I were the straight people, and all these marvelous things happened around us. I don't know how far it's gotten, but people like to say that it's something of a cult show.

"I loved playing Joshua, the father of Barnabas. I loved it when Jonathan and I used to really chew the scenery. By this time we had become quite good friends. He had a lot of classical training, like me, and we carried on like two old classical actors.

"It reminded me of an MGM movie with the costumes and sets. I usually enjoyed whatever they used me for. I remember in the very end I was a butler for the Collins family. I had never played a butler before, and I was so tickled to do it."

Edmonds has mixed memories of making the films based on the series, "I don't think it was a happy time for us, because it had to do with labor relations. The actors felt they were forced into doing it and were afraid they'd lose their jobs if they didn't. The monetary thing was another factor. We didn't make anything if the film made a profit. There were some amusing moments, however. On the first day Dan Curtis didn't know how to do anything, but look how far he's come."

Many of those involved with the **Dark Shadows** series feel the show went off the air because Dan Curtis lost interest. "He lost interest in it, and by that time he had set his sights on doing what he has become. The work was effected and so were the stories. They would introduce new characters and then they were disposed of. There was no continuity. They ran out of gimmicks and tricks. They ran out of areas to work in.

"I think (the continued interest in **Dark Shadows** is) wonderful for the little darlings, only I can't share their enthusiasm at all. It's as simple as that. It probably has to do with my success on *All My Children*, but I certainly have feelings of affection for those years on **Dark Shadows**. It broke ground."

By Edward Gross

GRAYSON HALL

*While **Dark** Shadows lives on in the hearts of its fans, several principle actors have, unfortunately, passed away. These individuals include Thayer David, who portrayed Professor Timothy Stokes; Joel Crothers, who essayed the part of Joe Haskall; and Grayson hall, one of the most popular actresses on the series, who breathed life into the role of Dr. Julia Joffman, the only person besides Willie Loomis who knew that Barnabas was a vampire.*

I was fortunate enough to interview Grayson Hall in what was probably her last interview. And for arranging the interview, I'm extremely grateful to her husband, Sam Hall, who served as one of DS' head writers. I will allow the talented actress to speak for herself.

ON BECOMING AN ACTRESS:

I always wanted to be an actress. I guess I didn't want to be who I was, and God knows I didn't know who I was. I guess the reason I finally became an actress was to leave home, to come and do something. I came to get away from my family and whoever I was. So I became an actress.

ON JOINING **DARK SHADOWS**:

It was the summer. I remember Sam and Matthew, our son, went to Ohio to see Sam's family. Something kept me here, I don't know what, but I came in the house and peeled my clothes off. I was lying in the air-conditioned splendor of the bedroom and my agent called me. He said, "Would

you like to do a soap? It's a thirteen week contract. You'll be a doctor, the vampire will find you out and you'll be killed, and that's the end of that." I said, "Great, a soap would be great." What happened is that I played this doctor filled with all these technical things that I had to talk about, and to make it not so dry I made a decision all by myself that I would be in love with him (Barnabas).

It wasn't written. I just kind of looked at him longingly. It just made it more interesting for me as a subtext. I don't know if you know anything about subtext. It's like you're talking to me and there's a whole thought process going through your mind about your next question. It's like when you're playing a character. So I decided that instead of being a serious dedicated doctor, I would be a serious dedicated doctor in love with a patient; a patient who happened to be a vampire.

Anyway, I did that and I think all the women across the country who were all madly in love with the vampire identified with me because I was in the position of touching him and talking to him. Mail started coming in and they kept me on. It was a valuable character, because I lived in the big house with Joan Bennett and all those people, and I had access to the house Barnabas lived in. So I

was in both places, as opposed to Willie, who was only in the Old House. There was value in the character to help keep his secret and all that stuff. About six or eight months later, Sam met Dan Curtis and was asked to write the show, which, after some hesitation, he agreed to do. Our lives were totally tied up with **Dark Shadows**. It was fascinating.

ON **DARK SHADOWS**:

I went to the studio after I spoke to my agent and met Bob Costello and Dan Curtis. You know, I suppose, that the character was supposed to be Dr. Julian Hoffman. I told Dan that I was interested and said, "When do I begin?" They brought me into the rehearsal room where the actors were waiting for whoever was going to play Hoffman. We rehearsed at 4:30 or five in the afternoon, and I was back at eight in the morning. I came here, called Sam and said, "Guess what's happening?" It started quicker than I had time to think about.

ON FANS:

I remember the funniest fan letter. I was after I had said, "Bite me, bite me," and Barnabas didn't want to, but he did want to bite Nancy Barrett. An angry letter said, "Dear Dr. Hoffman, how dare you let Barnabas bite Carolyn. You should be ashamed of yourself. I know this is only a story, but I hope you lose your license." Isn't that the best? It's called juggling reality with fantasy. I think that happens to an awful lot of people who are hooked on soaps...certainly **Dark Shadows**.

There's one fan that's very pushy. I don't think he's scary, but I've never met him. He's very pushy in an odd way. I guess the first time I heard from him was at the Martin Beck Theatre. It was after the half hour and I got a phone call at quarter to eight. It was across the stage and I was scared, wondering what was wrong. I said, "Hello," and a voice said, "Grayson, it's me." "What do you want?" "I just wanted to chat with you." "Idiot, how could you call me back stage?" I hung up, but then he got my home phone number. Very bizarre.

ON HER FAVORITE **DARK SHADOWS** ROLE:

I enjoyed playing Magda during the 1897 sequence. That was just so wild. It was my favorite.

ON RATINGS:

Soap operas are done so you only need to see them two or three times a week. If you missed a day of **Dark Shadows**, forget it. That's what happened. Dan insisted on making the show more complex. If it had been kept logical, it would have run forever.

ON FUNNY MOMENTS:

I remember it was nearly time to tape and during the countdown...the opening shot was Jonathan in his coffin. Just as the count got to one, Jonathan sat up and said, "Now, listen, I just want to say that I've been complaining for four years that this coffin is too short." We all fell down. He said, "Look at how I am. My knees have to be this way. I've got to have a larger coffin."

ON THE FILMS:

It was the same plot we had done on the show, but Barnabas killed me. The other one was supposed to star Jonathan, but he wouldn't do it. Sam and Dan had a hard time coming up with a story for **Night of Dark Shadows**. A werewolf isn't nearly as interesting as a vampire, and the only threat they could deal with was Angelique.

By Ken Friedmann

JERRY LACY

Jerry Lacy played the several roles on **Dark Shadows**, most unique among them being the role of Reverend Trask. "I really enjoyed playing the part," he recalls. "Trask really believed in what he was doing. He was convinced he was doing the world good, in what he did. I have to take that back a little, because there were different Trasks, and each one was a little different. Gregory Trask was not quite as straightforward and honest as the 1795 Trask. He was a fanatic, but he believed in what he was doing. . .and that makes it easy to play that type of character. It's not phony then. You're just absolutely convinced that this is the right way to do things.

"There are a lot of people in the world today, you may have noticed, who go around doing all sorts of things in the name of righteousness. I think Trask was a good example of that type of person."

Lacy was in the middle of a summer stock play in Middletown, Virginia when David Ford and Nancy Barrett came down to do a show called *Physicists*. He understudied David's part because he had to travel back and forth to New York to do some episodes of DS. Through this acquaintance, David eventually recommended him for a part on the show. "This was several months later, and I had in the meantime moved to Pennsylvania, where I was doing stock at the Allenbury Playhouse. I had written them a note asking them to come down and see the show if they had time. Instead, David phoned me and asked if I could come to New York to audition for Dan Curtis. I did, and got the part of Tony Peterson, a lawyer. Even then, there was too much emphasis on the Bogart as-

pect, and I think that hurt the character. He never amounted to very much, and I'm sure a lot of people don't even remember him. That was the first character I played on the show, and when we went into the past shortly afterwards, I began playing Reverend Trask (1795). It was totally a non-Bogart character, and it gave me an opportunity to develop something for myself, with some success.

" I guess the thing that comes first to my mind is the hard work. It was very hard work because Dan Curtis usually only used four or five main actors in any one script, so that the memorization chores were heavy. Especially if you were Reverend Trask and you had to learn all of those incantations and prayers; things that weren't normal dialogue. Dialogue is always easier to learn, but those things were really tough. I remember the fans outside the studio door waiting for you to come out at the end of the day. There would be 30, 40, 80. . .even 100 people out there. It was a big surprise to me, the popularity of the show. I remember the sets. The first time that I was sitting in the living room of Collinwood, and I'd only been on the show a few days, and it was between rehearsals. Some of us were sitting around taking a break and I was surprised to see a panel open in the back wall, and a

stage hand come through. I did a double-take because I didn't realize the secret panel was there. It's a lot of fun working with secret panels and ghosts and vampires."

As with any show where magic seems to strike such as on **Star Trek**, the cast of **Dark Shadows** all became quite fond of each other. Their mutual chemistry projected onto the screen. Lacy notes he "liked different people for different reasons and enjoyed working with everyone in the cast who was professional and competent. I looked forward to doing scenes with those people . DS, of course, did have a few people who were a little eccentric and had a few personality problems, shall we say; but all in all, it was a good experience. I supposed there were a few people I liked better than others, but that's true of any group. I still enjoy seeing them at the DS conventions.

"I really enjoyed being on the show. That kind of show is non-existent today, and even at the time 14 years ago , there wasn't anything else like it. Actors don't get a a chance to play that kind of melodrama much. From that point of view, it was very exciting. It was a big hit show, and it was a lot of fun. It was hard work but a lot of fun."

Every actor makes decisions in their career they live to regret. Oftentimes it is a role offered but not taken. Lacy is no exception. "There was one job offer that I turned down and that was to do scenes of Shakespeare at the Old Globe Theater in San Diego. I had to make my living in Los Angeles at the time, and I could not afford to go there. I think if I had to do it all over, I probably would have gone and figured out how I was going to eat when I got there.

"It would have been difficult for me to turn down a Broadway show, even though I think, perhaps, it may have been a good idea if I hadn't done Bogart, since I've had so much trouble since. At the time, there was no way I could have said no to it. Another thing is I probably wouldn't have stayed so long on *Love of Life*. I now think I perhaps should have left earlier than I did. That probably would have been better."

Oftentimes an actor and their role begin to resemble each other, at least on some points. "Reverend Trask," Lacy says, "was very zealous. He really put himself into everything he did, and he was going to get it down come hell or high water. There is some of that in me. When I set out to do something, I'm going to get it done. . .move rocks, mountains, to do it. Of course, Trask cheated, lied, murdered to get what he wanted, and I draw the line at those things. The only thing I share with Trask is the incredible need to put the finger on vampires and werewolves, because I'm always keeping an eye out for them. You never know where one is going to show up. You have to be very careful."

Jerry Lacy and Joan Bennett.

By Edward Gross

"My name is Victoria Winters...I am going on a journey that will bring me to a strange, dark house on the edge of the sea at

ALEXANDRA MOLTKE

Widow's Hill...a journey to link my past with my future; a journey that is bringing me closer to a world I've never known...to darkness and strangeness that I hope will open the doors of life to me. A journey to people I've never met; people who, tonight, are still only shadows in my mind, but who will soon fills the days and nights of my tomorrow."

Among the first passages of dialogue spoken on the very first episode of **Dark Shadows**, this established right off the bat that the focal point of the series was Victoria Winters; that everything that happened would either directly or indirectly effect her. It was an integral part of the soap, and a search went out for just the right actress to essay the role. She was found in the persona of Alexandra Moltke.

"I was told that I was the only innocent looking actress in New York," Moltke laughs, "and that's how I got the part. I had to try several times, and then I had a screen test for the role. Oddly enough, on the screen test I looked like Joan Bennett, which I wasn't supposed to, but that added a whole new element to the story, which they resolved later on, that I was supposed to be her illegitimate daughter. I don't even remember, it was all done in one day."

Moltke attributes her career as an actress to the fact that she was "bad" in just about everything else she tried in school. Acting, she felt, was an outlet for her feelings.

"Once," she recalls, "in my ju-

nior year, I got into a lot of trouble and was kicked out of the play that we were doing. I was so upset about that, that I realized how much I wanted to be an actress. So it turned out to be a good thing. I went to acting school after that. I got started in acting when an agent came to the acting school where I was and picked me out of the play."

From the very first day, she was quite enthusiastic about her role on the series.

"I really enjoyed working on a show that had so much imagination, and I also enjoyed making friends. It was a real family in the beginning, because it was such a great adventure and that was a very happy experience. Then there was the craziness and humor that went with it. I also enjoyed the salary. I probably admired Joan Bennett the most on the show. She is very professional and she always kept a good humor about her, because sometimes things were delayed and unorganized, as you can imagine on a show like that with all the special effects. She was unfailing in her self-discipline and she was a very good example to the rest of us."

The lack of organization often made its way onto the television screen in the show's infamous on-air bloopers.

"There are quite a few," Moltke

smiles. "I was responsible for a couple that had to be re-taped. There was one day when two actors were, shall we say, under the weather, doing a scene together they hadn't bothered to memorize. They decided that they would wing it on the teleprompter. We were taping and they were reading their scenes very well off the teleprompter, when suddenly one of them realized that he was speaking the other person's lines, and vice versa, and they just had to plunge on ahead, making no sense whatsoever. Of course those of us on the side were hysterical."

While she admits that there were too many characters on the series for her to pick a favorite, when pressed Moltke mentions the late Thayer David, perhaps best known as Professor Timothy Stokes on the show.

"I suppose the Barnabas character was a favorite, and the Frankenstein one [Adam]," she explains, "but, oh God, anything Thayer played he made very special. That's a good point, because oft-times it was what the actor had done with the character. Clarice Blackburn was wonderful as the housekeeper and she made that character more memorable than some of the actors who were on for a more steady basis."

The passage of years may cloud some memories, but the actress is quick to point out that a typical day on the set stands out so clearly that it seems to have occurred only yesterday, rather than twenty years ago.

"I don't remember the beginning of the day very well, because I always arrived in a state of fog," Moltke smiles sheepishly. "Most of us, of course, had not learned our lines the night before, so we would try to bluff our way through. It was very much like going to school when you haven't done your homework. We did blocking upstairs. Perhaps we had blocked some work out the night before. So we would stagger through that for an hour and a half or so, and then it would be time for make-up and hair. We never had a lunch break. Make-up was probably *considered* our lunch break. Then we'd have to go down to the floor, and there really wasn't very much in the way of air. It was all very gray and enormous. It got to be very cozy, because wherever the action was in the studio, it was always very lively.

"It was with three cameras," she elaborates. "Whenever we had a special effect, forget about rehearsing, because that took a lot of time. We'd have little breaks every now and then, and then I guess we'd run through a dress rehearsal and then tape. We were always nervous every day, because although it wasn't live, it was treated as though it were live. We would never go back and re-tape. I'm very nearsighted and I couldn't see the teleprompter and I think that almost everybody in the cast was nearsighted."

Moltke believes part of Jonathan Frid's appeal as Barnabas had to do with the fact that he could not see the teleprompter very well.

"That faraway look that Barnabas used to get," she laughs, "was really a desperate searching for the teleprompter. However, a whole other personality developed out of that. People thought that he was just a lost, unhappy, well meaning vampire when, in fact, he wasn't supposed to be that way at all. Then we would tape. We would have a half hour break and we'd start it again. If you were working two days consecutively, it was a day that ran from 8 AM to 6 PM, which is quite a long day to be standing on a concrete floor without fresh air. It was quite tiring, although the only real strain came during taping. It kind of built up through the course of the day."

The "strain" apparently took its toll on the actress, as she left the

series during its third year and was replaced by Betsy Durkin for a short time before the character of Victoria Winters was dropped altogether. Moltke's reason for her departure was attributed to what she calls "an act of God."

"I suppose an act of God can mean many things," she points out, "but in my case it meant that I was pregnant, and I had some very heavy things to do; difficult things I had to do, and I wasn't having a very easy time with my pregnancy. So I had to get out, legally, from my contract, because they didn't seem to want to let me out. As a matter of fact, *Rosemary's Baby* had just come out at that time, and I was terrified that they'd want to keep me all the way through."

This fear was not paranoia, as the idea of Victoria Winters giving birth to the child of Satan was not that outlandish an idea, a fact that writer Sam Hall can attest to.

"We had indexes of horror stories," Hall concurs, "and we all read Wilke Collins until we were jumping out of our skins. We did

the werewolf, Frankenstein and so many others. Dan Curtis would come in and say, 'I just read this. Steal it,' whether it made any sense or not in terms of the characters."

And so Moltke left before her child was given over to the devil. When the series finally left the air in 1971, she admits that she felt it a sad moment.

"I'm sorry that it went off the air," concludes Moltke, "because I think there was nothing else on that time of day that stretched people's imagination and humor the way that that show did. It was a real fantasy escape and it seemed to help an awful lot of people. Nobody has taken chances like that, and I think it's really to Dan Curtis' credit that a show like that was put on and that he was responsible for it. I miss the series. It was the funniest show on television, although we didn't always see the comedy that everybody else did."

STAR PANEL

Joan Bennett, Jonathan Frid, Marie Wallace, Terryayne Crawford and Donna Wandrey at the Dark Shadows Festival, Newark, New Jersey, 1985 as transcribed by Julie Illescas

Master of Ceremonies - Jeff Thompson

JEFF:

We'd like to welcome two beloved **Dark Shadows** stars, Miss Joan Bennett and Mr. Jonathan Frid.

(Both enter to a standing ovation).

AUDIENCE:

Jonathan, after DS was cancelled you seemed to drop out of sight for several years. Where were you?

JONATHAN:

Well, I just went to bed. Just goofed off and had a lovely time. I worked a little bit off and on in a couple of movies that weren't too professional, and I did some dinner theater out West, and then disappeared off to Mexico and had a lovely time there for awhile, went up to Canada and came back. However, you're going to see more of me in the future, starting with my one-man show, Reflections of Evil, that I hope you'll all see tomorrow. I want to turn that into a professional presentation in the New Year. (Editor's Note: Of course Jonathan has been very successful in this endeavor and "Fools and Fiends", successor to "Reflections of Evil," is now on national tour). Meanwhile, I appreciate you people for being such marvelous trial audiences. Without these Festivals I probably would never have done this. So I'll be eternally grateful for your support of this show, but it's the future that I want to talk about today.

AUDIENCE:

Jonathan, how did you like playing a vampire?

Joan Bennett as Elizabeth Collins Stoddard in DARK SHADOWS

JONATHAN:

Wish I'd known my lines better. I was a nervous wreck most of the time, but vampires are nervous wrecks, too, so the one played into the other.

AUDIENCE:

Miss Bennett, we all enjoyed your performance on DS, and I'm sure everyone here would agree we're very grateful to you for coming. Thank you very much.

JOAN:

Thank you.

AUDIENCE:

Miss Bennett, in the beginning of the show before Barnabas came into it, the show was more or less a typical soap opera, mystery plots and everything, but when Barnabas came into it, it took a supernatural turn. What were your feelings on that?

JOAN:

I was delighted. Not only with the character, but with Jonathan himself.

JONATHAN:

I took over some of the work load. In fact, I felt the same way when David Selby came on. I said to Dan, "You've got to get somebody else on this show. Another Monster to help take some of the weight off me, as well as help me!" Apart from any thoughts of competition, I was delighted that they gave me a break there for awhile.

AUDIENCE:

Miss Bennett, I hear you're still in contact with Alexandra (Moltke) Isles. If you could possibly give her a message from all of us, send her our love and tell her we miss her.

JOAN:

I shall deliver the message.

AUDIENCE:

Miss Bennett, what was it like working with Spencer Tracy in *Father of the Bride*?

JOAN:

Great. He was one of my favorite actors. (Gives Jonathan a quick look.) *One* of them.

AUDIENCE:

I've really enjoyed all the movies that you've done, especially *Father of the*

Bride. How did it feel to be almost chosen for the Scarlett O'Hara part in *Gone With the Wind*?

JOAN:

I was a little sorry to have lost it.

AUDIENCE:

Jonathan, in most of the series you always played Barnabas Collins, but everybody else played different people. How did you remember which character each was playing?

MARIE:

Sometimes he didn't!

JONATHAN:

Well, it was easy for me because I always forgot what happened the day before anyway. I just played what they gave me that day and if I could keep *that* much going I was lucky.

AUDIENCE:

Miss Bennett, what did you do after DS was cancelled?

JUAN:

I did summer stock in "Butterflies are Free." A lot of summer stock...winter stock....

AUDIENCE:

Miss Bennett, how do you feel about the current process of adding color to black and white films, and also, do you have any anecdotes concerning your sister Constance Bennett?

JOAN:

I haven't seen any of the color. I was talking to Ruth Warrick about it last night and she was explaining how it was done. She said maybe that's why Louis Edmonds had pink hair. My sister and I were good friends, but I can't think of any anecdotes.

AUDIENCE:

Miss Bennett, do you have plans to make another film or TV appearance?

JOAN:

No, I haven't.

AUDIENCE:

Did you ever get tired of going up and down those stairs?

JOAN:

Yes.

AUDIENCE:

Could you say something about what you remember of your childhood in Fort Lee?

JOAN:

It wasn't in Fort Lee. I was born in Palisades, but we moved to New York when I was about three, so I don't remember too much.

AUDIENCE:

Do you have any favorite roles?

JOAN:

Motion pictures, you mean? *Scarlet Street*, *Woman in the Window*.

AUDIENCE:

What was it like working with Fritz Lang?

JOAN:

Most people didn't get along with him because he was pretty severe, but I got along with him beautifully and I think he was a wonderful director.

MARIE:

Excuse me, I have a question for Jonathan Frid. Why did you walk across the credits wearing your underwear?

JONATHAN:

It wasn't that at all. I was wearing very respectable outer garments. What happened was, we used to have a little cubbyhole behind the place that led to Mrs. Johnson's quarters or the kitchens or whatever under that staircase. We used to have a little change room there if we had changes from one set to another. Sometimes a day would pass in one episode so you had to have a change of clothes. That's where I used to make my changes occasionally, but they usually had these areas roped off whenever they decided to take one set and use that for the background for the credits, but they didn't think to rope off the little dressing room back there. I didn't know, and as soon as I came through I heard them say, "Get back, get back, bet back!"

AUDIENCE:

How badly would the scene have to fall apart before you stopped the tape?

JONATHAN:

Well, it had to be pretty bad. Obviously you've seen some pretty messy things that never got retaken. I think maybe once or twice I just quit. I said, "I give up. I'm totally confused at this point. I don't know what I'm saying." Or you might use some profanity and they'd have to stop. But normally they didn't do it. Nowadays they do it, apparently. They make soaps now like movies. I mean, retake and retake, and they do them out of sequence. Just like a movie. But in those days, it cost several hundreds — if not thousands of dollars — to make an edit. I might just say at this point one of my very favorite scenes was during the 1795 period. It was when I came in and Josette has married Jeremiah. That comes off rather well now as you see it. I wanted to do it beautifully and perfectly, and I went up. It was awful. It was so awful.

JOAN:

They probably don't know what 'going up' means.

JONATHAN:

Going up means forgetting my lines. So anyway, I said to Robert Costello — Robert wanted me to meet some people that day from ABC — and I said to him, "if you would, I would love to get this scene edited tonight. Can I go over with Jack Sullivan—who had to do this every night—to the editing room at ABC." They put in other things besides just editing bloopers. I said, "I'll meet these people, but please do this one thing for me," and he said OK. There must have been three or four men over there, after hours, working for about two hours. I don't know what it cost him, but anyway, I had a lot of fun with suggesting editing. I don't know how to do it, but I know that you take the sound out of the soundtrack and you separate the soundtrack from the videotrack and you play around. We eliminated that awful hole and the scene finally worked. But that's the only time that I can remember where I really interfered. I begged them. They weren't happy, but they let it go. It was very, very costly to do that, and they preferred not to.

AUDIENCE:

Miss Bennett, what was your favorite character?

JOAN:

My favorite character was Elizabeth.

AUDIENCE:

I have a question for Marie and Donna and Terry. Do you remember a favorite scene that you played with Miss Bennett?

MARIE:

Yes! When I tried to kill you.

DONNA:

I can remember the first time I got bitten. Miss Bennett said for three days running, "Don't worry, you'll be fine," and here the blood is coming out. . .

TERRAYNE:

I can't compete with that!

AUDIENCE:

Mr. Frid, who came up with the idea for that haircut?

JONATHAN:

Since Bob Costello himself admitted to this last year when he was here, I guess I'm not saying anything behind his back. He had to pose for that portrait in the hall because they had to have it ready before they even got an actor for Barnabas. They had to have everything done but the face, so as soon as they got the actor they could put in the face. So Bob posed for it, and he sort of doesn't have too much hair, and what hair he has he pulled across his forehead into bangs. We often kidded about it. That's how I ended up with having the bangs. It became, of course, one of the trademarks of the character.

AUDIENCE:

I think the character of Barnabas ranks right up there with those of the best horror actors, Boris Karloff and Bela Lugosi.

JONATHAN:

That's in pretty good company. The two actors that I grew up with that were in the horror genre were Boris Karloff and Bela Lugosi. I did see Lugosi as a vampire when I was young, but I think Boris Karloff's roles probably influenced anything I did with my vampire roles rather than Bela Lugosi. Bela Lugosi — to watch his show is fascinating. It's like a ballet, and it makes me think the story of Dracula would make a beautiful ballet, if not an opera. Lugosi, the way he slides up and down those staircases. It was beautiful, so slow motion.

AUDIENCE:

How many days prior to air time did you tape an episode?

MARIE:

Approximately one week.

JONATHAN:

Each one was done by itself every day. Live tape. It's kind of a contradiction of terms.

AUDIENCE:

Because of the characters that you played — particularly the evil ones — did any of you every have any problems with sales people or the general public?

JONATHAN:

Come on, evil ladies, speak up!

MARIE:

It's funny. I enjoyed playing evil people, and would meet people outside who would say, "You're terrific! You're so bad!" So it didn't seem to hurt me. Only then, when I played crazy Jenny....Once when I was walking on the street....I thought my crazy Jenny characterization with the hair and everything was so different than I am. I mean, I put little rollers in my hair over here, I teased my hair out to here, I wore false lashes on top and bottom. I put dark shadows in here and everything. I looked absolutely crazy. And one day I'm walking on 42nd Street near Lexington Avenue, and someone said to me, "Hey! You're crazy Jenny!" And I said, "How did you know?" And she said, "You look just like you do on television!"

DONNA:

One wonderful woman on a bus once picked up her cane and slugged me with it. I had started going out with Trask. She screamed at the top of her lungs, "YOU SLUT!" I have played such nice women for my entire career....She was furious. I got off the bus, I walked. That was it. If she's here today, I turned out OK. Don't believe those parts we play.

TERRYAYNE:

I only had one day as a vampire, and my character, Beth, I can't see her really being an evil lady. The only 'evil' character I played was Edith Collins for a short while. For me it was a very one-dimensional character. I thought I was just yelling all the time. The fans outside said, "Please, Beth, will you come back as Beth? Please, we like Beth, we don't like her. Please come back as Beth."

AUDIENCE:

Mr. Frid, will you tell us your first impressions of meeting Joan Bennett when you first started on the show?

JONATHAN:

Oh, I was terrified. I was in awe. Of course, they were all quite a little group, you know, by that time. I was in very formidable company. But all my fears and awe of all these marvelous people that I was working with played into Barnabas beautifully, because he was scared out of his wits. In a few days I found they were all very nice people. Joan was a dear to work with. After a few days of getting over all the awe of Hollywood and everything, I had a lovely time during the four years we worked together.

AUDIENCE:

How does the panel feel about the current resurgence of popularity of the show?

JONATHAN:

I have a marvellous answer for that. Last year I said we had a sort of cult following. Now we've become a part of American folklore.

Thank you very much to our guests!

By Edward Gross

JOHN SEDWICK

Dark Shadows had a limited number of directors. Primary among them were Lela Swift, Henry Kaplan and John Sedwick, all of whom played an important role in shaping **Dark Shadows** and allowing it to transcend time.

"Those of us who were connected with it, especially at the beginning, felt that we were doing something different in daytime," says director John Sedwick. "Television had not done a mystery-ghost-vampire soap opera before. The soaps usually centered around problems at home, and love problems. **Dark Shadows** was sort of a new experiment. It actually started as a Nancy Drew-type mystery. We did have some ghosts, but it wasn't until Barnabas arrived nine months into the series that it caught fire. A lot of that was due to the character and the actor, Jonathan Frid, who portrayed him, as well as the bizarre concept of a vampire.

"We found out early that when we got to the vampire stage, we could not comment on it. We could not camp it up. It had to be treated like he was a real vampire living in a real mansion like Collinwood. We had to play it very real without camping it up and making comments on the acting. We had to take this bizarre situation and make it very real for the public. We couldn't do what *Batman* did with the POWS! and ZAPS! If he bit somebody, it was as though he would do it in normal life. That was one of the saving graces that made the show as successful as it was."

Sam Hall has said that Jonathan Frid was not Dan Curtis' first choice to play Barnabas. Sedwick believes otherwise but isn't certain, "I never heard that, but we had little to do with the casting. Jonathan played it very honestly.

He had a wonderful mysterious sort of quality...a larger-than-life quality. He could look evil and exude this vampire-undead mystique. I think Jonathan had a great time playing it. He was one of the few people who didn't mind lying in a casket. He spent a lot of time in one, but after all that was his bed on the show. He didn't mind, but several others did. One of the girls, Kathryn Leigh Scott, had to get into a casket once. She was going to have a nightmare in which she dreamed of seeing herself in a casket, and so we had to get a shot of her in it. She gritted her teeth, closed her eyes and lay back in the casket. We got a quick shot, she got out and was really off the wall...really spooked by having to lie in a casket. Jonathan just sort of played around and had a great time.

"He enjoyed playing Barnabas, and he had a magnitude about him. He had a very great presence when he was just looking, watching. He had great eyes and good thinking contact as an actor. His mouth even had a smile, a sort of evil little twitch or twist that was very interesting."

Everyone knows what became of **Dark Shadows** after the arrival of Barnabas Collins. But what was the series like before his arrival. Veteran Sedwick comments, "It was sort of a tame murder mystery

filled with dark shadows. We had a murder, as I recall, and the ghost of a seaman came back. The first nine months there wasn't all that much happening. I think they might have had another six months to see what they could do. It really caught fire with Barnabas.

"For one thing, it was a show that flashed back to 1795, where it had a whole different look. The show had an awfully good look. We had a set designer named Sy Tomashoff, and an art director named Mel Handleman on lighting. Between the two of them we had a look which was fantastic. The sets and props were wonderful. The show itself was wonderful, because there was the hand coming out of the coffin. I mean, how many times do you do that in a career? We had a lot of effects. It was early in the chromokey days and we did the shows like a live show. You'd mark the acting and the camera very carefully with the chromokey background. With this you have to tape it right then and there, because if you move at all, it's going to be off.

One of my favorite sequences is when we had to hang this young man. he was Vicky Winters' boyfriend back in time. She was hung and then he was hung because they were witches or something. We did this full hanging sequence in one shot. We had a scaffolding and the rope was around this young man's neck, and there were two guards with him. One asked if he had any last words and he said no and the black sack was put over his head, with the noose being placed around his neck."

Sedwick continues, "As we panned down the body, we saw his hands, which were theoretically tied behind his back, though they weren't. We gave a cue to one of the guards to tap the guy with the black mask, and he in turn would grab hold of the scaffolding. The camera kept panning down until we got to his feet, which were on a step ladder type arrangement. We cued the guard to make sure he had a good grip and then the ladder was kicked out from under him. His feet kind of bounced and dropped a little bit. He wiggled somewhat and it was all most effective. It was rather ghoulish, but, I think, quite effective."

Sedwick recalls some of the more amusing moments on the series. "Unfortunately there were no out-takes of this because we could only see it on the off air camera, but when Barnabas had to bite a young damsel on the neck to draw his weekly or daily quota of blood, you would see him approaching the girl...we always had to have a very tight cutaway shot of the girl looking frightened, and while we were on the tight shot of the girl, the camera was on Barnabas. He reached into his pocket, pulled out his fangs, put them in his mouth, turned back to the girl and sort of snarled and got his mouth in position. That was his cue for me to get back on him, and he'd bite her. That was an off the air camera, so we have no tapes of it, but it was so funny to watch.

Another event Sedwick remembers was not quite so amusing for all involved. "Jonathan had an awful lot to do," Sedwick notes, "and some days he was slower learning his part. One time he was strangling Grayson Hall and he forgot his line, which was, 'I'm going to kill you.' He's strangling her and strangling her when Grayson, who'd realized that he had forgotten his line, said, 'You're not going to *kill* me, are you?' He replied, 'Oh yes, I'm going to kill you.'"

Writers and directors for **Dark Shadows** worked under enormous pressures. Sedwick remembers some of these. "I was there for two years and ran into artistic problems a couple of times. If he (Curtis) insisted, I would have to do it. There was a lot of pressure on the show because there were so many technical things. It started off as a weekly effect of some

sort, then biweekly and then day to day; you found yourself spending more time working out the technicalities than working with the actors. There was a lot of pressure to make the effects work."

What's it like living in the middle of a phenomenon? Just when does it dawn on a director that he is part of a national cult? Sedwick explains, "About nine months after the Barnabas story was introduced, we realized it was catching on. We saw the ratings and the response from the kids. One time somebody published where we taped the show and soon the area was crowded with kids waiting for autographs.

"(Dark Shadows) is entertainment. It's why you go to the movies. You enjoy the actors and you want to see somebody with more troubles than you have. In a soap you get interested in their daily lives because it's five times a week and you get to know these people. The audience many times has a mixed belief in who the real people are...they know it's a show, but the audience gets mixed up between the actors and the characters. On *Guiding Light* there's someone making threatening calls to either the actors or the characters. Sometimes you get them to the character and they say that the producer knows what's happening and they're going to get him if he doesn't change things. They look at the character as a real person, yet they know it's a TV show. I think there's a lot of problems with soap operas in being recognized. You can't go to the store without people wanting your autograph. Sometimes, if you're playing a bad guy, you can get hit or slapped in the face. There's a problem with the actors not being able to go out in public."

Adding a vampire to the cast of a show is not a traditional move in soap opera production. Sedwick says, "The show had been 'ghostly' before that, but he was a bigger ghost. It was rather tricky to do the ghost, by the way. We needed two cameras. You needed a background, then an actor on another

set against black, so you could superimpose the two images together. Now that background has to be out of focus, because the wall behind the ghost would be seen through the ghost and you'd need a soft focus. Then if you wanted to tighten in on the ghost, you had to coordinate two cameras tightening at the same time, or it would look terrible. It worked, although it took time to do it. I think the effects got even crazier after I left. It took a lot of effort to make it work as best we could. I left the series just before Quentin came on.

"I was spending so much time trying to work out the special effects that I wasn't doing what I liked to do, which was to work with the actors and to work in something more dramatic than effects. Plus I was getting a little tired of it, and was ready for a change. Some people were getting on my nerves. Also, towards the end it got too crazy. The final storyline was that they were in the present, yet they could see their lives in the future. Now this is hard to do in a controlled two hour dramatic film or play, so certainly on a daily basis it's awfully hard to handle. Dan repeated the Barnabas story in different time periods, and it wore thin."

Sedwick concludes by saying, "It was very interesting and rewarding. I learned a hell of a lot, and I wanted to do something different so I changed. It was a rare experience. Professionally, it was very interesting and a very valuable learning experience.

"It was an interesting period in television, though I wish it had lasted longer."

RON SPROUT

By Edward Gross

Like all other soap operas, **Dark Shadows** had a substantial list of writers who labored to deliver the terrors to thrill audiences each weekday afternoon. **DS**, though, was tougher to write than most others because it went through an enormous amount of material very quickly.

Considering this, it's actually surprising the series didn't use up more writers than it did, as many them stayed with the series for several years. One of the heartiest was Ron Sproat, whose involvement began in the early pre-Barnabas days and lasted to the point when they introduced David Selby as Quentin Collins.

"When I came on," says Sprout, "It was following Art Wallace's story, which was mainly centered around Joan Bennett. The character, Elizabeth Collins-Stoddard turned out to be a lady who had murdered her husband and had him buried in the basement. She was a recluse now. Then the governess, Victoria Winters, came in. She was in charge of a cannery and the man who was her foreman, Bill Malloy, was murdered. Vicky was drawn into that. A character named Burke Devlin was set up as an antagonist of the Collins family. She thought he had done it. That's when I came on the show, and there was also the body buried in the basement. So there were two storylines, a murder story, a body in the basement and also, at that time, there was much more made about Vicky's identity. She was an orphan. Was she the daughter of Elizabeth? It was hinted heavily that she was. That's what was happening.

"Dan had always wanted to get into the supernatural, but I think he was a little afraid at the beginning. He had footage he had shot on location for the waves breaking against the shore, the houses and all that. He had shot footage of Kathryn Leigh Scott with a mask over her face, running in and out of some columns, looking very ghostly. I saw that and thought it was wonderful. It was an eerie kind of fun. The first time there was a ghost on the show was when we decided the Thayer David character was done in by a ghost. Then a ghost saved Vicky at the Old House. Then it seemed like that ought to be continued. It also seemed like a letdown after the excitement. The next day we used that footage of Kathryn running in and out of the pillars. In calming down Vicky, Elizabeth told her a story about some resident ghost named Josette, who later turned up. All of this stuff seemed to be working, and I loved doing it.

The audience loved it as well. Sprout explains, "The audience seemed to like that, but there wasn't much of an audience. The ratings went up a little bit. Before, the show had been done in long scenes, one long scene per act. We started splitting up the acts so that it had a more cinematic pace, cutting back and forth between two scenes, two places, and so on. When we started doing that, we started getting more excitement in the stories. This had all been worked out in advance. Dan also had footage of Matthew moving around the roof of Collinwood, pushing a pot off that almost hit Vicky. Obviously that had been thought of before. But once it got going that way, what had been plotted afterwards was a story about Roger's wife who was going to come back to claim David, which was going to run concurrently with a story about a sailor, Jason McGuire, who was coming back to blackmail Elizabeth. That's about as far as it had been plotted.

"The ratings had gone up a bit," Sprout continues, "but they were still quite low. The Matthew business and the stuff with the ghosts had helped them a little bit. The stories we were struck with were the blackmail story with the body buried in the basement, which was supposed to be the main story, and the story of the wife coming back to claim David in a custody suit.

"So we all went out to lunch and said, 'How can we resolve this? It just seems deadly dull.' We were having lunch that day with Dan (Curtis) and Bob Costello, and I think it was Dan who said, 'What if Roger's wife is dead?' So we said, 'Oh, that's much more fun. She's really not a living person. That's terrific.' We devised the plot that she was a Phoenix. Some scripts had been written before, talking about her and it turned out that she came from Phoenix, Arizona. So she's a Phoenix from Phoenix. At any rate, we started a story about the mother coming back for David, except that she wants to take him back to wherever she goes. She wanted him to die in fire. That seemed to build up the ratings enormously. I always dreaded the days that I had to write the Jason McGuire thing. But the Phoenix story ended with the fire. David was in the fire and Vicky saved him. By this time a writer named Malcolm Mormorstein was on the show, and he wrote the scene where she got him out of the fire. Then we were having a cousin come from England. It was another blackmail plot that had been projected. It was Dan Curtis who said, 'I want to go for broke. I want a vampire in there.'

"I loved it. I thought it was terrific. The only concern I voiced was, 'What are we going to do to top it?' It's real exciting and fun, and I love vampires. I just couldn't think of anything we could do after that which would top it. As it turned out, though, he stayed on the show until the end. At any rate, we did it and Dan said that this was Russian roulette. So we went with it and had lots of story meetings. I remember one meeting that lasted twenty seven hours, because we were fighting deadlines and making this stuff up. It was exciting and fun."

Sam Hall had indicated that Jonathan Frid was not Curtis' first choice for Barnabas. Spout says, "I don't think that's right. I know that during that time Dan and Bob Costello did the casting, and all I remember is that we were talking about where to go with this character, and one idea was for Bert Convy. They were thinking of a handsome vampire. The Frank Langella look. Dan didn't like that because it wasn't scary enough. All I know is that Dan handed me a picture of Jon and said, 'This is our new vampire.' I thought it was great, because Jonathan and I had gone to school together. Dan hated a lot of what we blocked out storywise, because it made Barnabas sympathetic. Dan never wanted him to be sympathetic. He hated it."

Curtis finally got his way with the vampire in the feature film **House of Dark Shadows**. Sprout recalls, "He finally said, 'You're going to do it *my* way.' We just felt we couldn't get that much mileage out of a character who is pure evil. It isn't interesting anyway.When you're dealing with two and a half hours a week and

you're seeing a lot of the character, it just has to have more dimension than that. Even the villain has to have different colors other than snarling and snapping. In fact, in the book *Dracula*, Dracula hardly appears at all. He's in the beginning and the end, but most of it's the search for him. Anyway, that's how that evolved. Our ratings started going up when the vampire came on.

"I think part of it is because [Jonathan] played a duality, and had kind of a lost quality as well. He said originally, and I think he was right, 'Don't write the evil. I'll play that. I look that way.' That's what he said. He also said that he'd done *Richard III*, and he was astounded by the reviews at the time, because they said he was the most evil Richard on record. He said, 'I was playing for sympathy.' So he suggested that we write *against* the evil and he would play against it, which would make it more interesting. That's what we did and I thought it worked.

Sprout explains that the Barnabas character was introduced only for thirteen weeks, after which he was expected to depart the series. "The idea was that after thirteen weeks he would be staked and then we'd go on to something else. What, we never knew. That's what worried me at the start of it. There was a great deal of excitement about a vampire and it just seemed to me that other things, like Frankenstein, just aren't as interesting.

"The ratings went way up, just steadily climbing. It seemed like people were saying, 'Hey, there's a show with a vampire.'

"The other characters weren't supposed to know what a vampire was. They never read about vampires or heard of them. It was as though it was something we had stumbled upon for the first time. The show did change tone violently. At one point there were many disagreements about how it should be handled. I thought it was going too campy. I thought it got kind of crazy at the point where you have

a witch, who has been transformed into a vampire, talking to a man-made man, who wants a man-made woman, and the devil is walking around telling everybody what to do. Then there was another vampire, plus there was a werewolf. I was throwing my hands up in despair at that time. I thought the whole 'Eve' plotline was absolute nonsense. She's a man-made woman who runs around the woods in an evening dress. I just thought it was silly. I thought it took the magic and fun out of it.

"Looking back on it, I thought there were other ways to handle it than the ways that were taken. There was a basic disagreement. I felt that it shouldn't be fantastic, that there should be some root in reality; some sort of bizarre reality. Another writer felt it should be total fantasy, total craziness.

"Not only did we have indexes on stories." Sprout continues, "but Dan insisted that we had to have something happen at the end of every act. There had to be some sort of horrific suspense to get you through the next act. As a result of that, things happened that were terrible. They bumped off a major character, Sam Evans, at the end of act two, and his daughter barely had time to say, 'My poor father died.'

"There came a point where no one knew what the hell was going on. We had arguments about that. I told Dan that I felt we owed a certain obligation to the person who isn't able to get to the television everyday, to explain what's going on. That we should keep a fairly clear storyline. Fans didn't want to have a guide that would untangle all of this. They were in the process of straightening it out a bit, and I think it was going pretty well about the time of Quentin." The point at which Sprout left the series.

One of the more fascinating, and unique, moments in the series was when the focus shifted to 1795 and the supporting cast played a second group of characters. Sprout was intimately involved in this segment. "Gordon and I both wanted to do that," he explains. "We had talked about it. It was actually my idea of just how to do it. Dan said, 'That's okay, but how do they do it?' I went home to think about it and he also asked how we would use the supporting cast. I came in and said, 'Why don't we use the supporting cast like this, they're the ancestors of the people on the show.' So it was kind of my idea, and a good one. I thought those episodes added freshness to the show, having the cast play different roles. I thought the costumes worked for it, and I liked the feel they gave the show. It was a terrible letdown to come back to mini-skirts.

"Angelique came up because we had to expand Barnabas. Obviously he was the most popular character in the show, so the thinking was one logical way to do it would be to find out how he became a vampire. Originally we were going to have it happen through ghosts and books rather than having her go all the way back to the past, but that worked out better. Once we worked out this thing of how to use the other people—that was what had stopped us previously—we decided to do it that way. So we had Angelique, and then we had to go back and find out why she would want to turn him into a vampire."

While crafting a show, a writer is too busy to often worry about his audience. Largely a writer writes to please his more direct management, the director and producer. Sprout recalls that he had little time to be concerned with who was watching his work. "It started getting a lot of attention, and the only way I knew that was by the kids who waited outside the studio, because they were there for the actors. They just kept growing and growing, and by the time that Adam came on, they used to wait for him. Kids really got into Robert Rodan.

"As a writer, I enjoyed working on it more than I had enjoyed working on anything else. It brought out a childlike exuberance that I don't think I experienced since I was a child myself, sitting around a campfire with other kids trying to out-scare each other. There was such fun in that, and we had fun doing it, and that kind of came across on the tube. The audience also thought it was the campiest thing they'd ever seen, and liked it for that reason. It got a little too campy for my taste. Some people tuned in to see what we would dare do next.

" I get a kick out of the fact that people get such an enjoyment out of something I'd done so long ago," Sprout concludes. "I was not aware of ratings or anything. My friends were talking about it and were hooked on it, which I thought was kind of nice. I had great fun writing it, and then suddenly we were getting interviewed by *The Times, Newsweek, Time*, and I just thought it was kind of a novelty. But I loved writing the show up to a point; up to the point where it got too campy. It also was a terrible crime, because Dan was there asking for it. We were constantly in meetings and under the gun, trying to come up with something where you had to have some kind of cliff-hanger every single day, and even cliff-hangers within the show. It was very, very hard to plot. It was constant work."

—DARK SHADOWS—

appendix: episodes

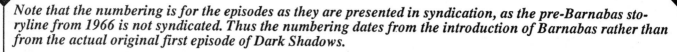

Note that the numbering is for the episodes as they are presented in syndication, as the pre-Barnabas storyline from 1966 is not syndicated. Thus the numbering dates from the introduction of Barnabas rather than from the actual original first episode of Dark Shadows.

EPISODE 1
Jason gets money from Liz to send Willie away from Collinwood, but Willie sneaks into the secret vault of the mausoleum and is terror stricken when he sees a hand reach out of the coffin he has opened.

EPISODE 2
Vicki sends David out to play and joins Liz, who has just met Barnabas Collins, the family's 175-year-old vampire—posing as a distant relative newly arrived from England. David is at play in the house house when Barnabas suddenly appears...and makes it quite clear that he knows the place very, very well.

EPISODE 3
[Storyline missing]

EPISODE 4
Who stole Willie's things? Willie himself? Jason suspects Burke; Burke suspects Jason. Disappointed to learn that Burke is not romantically interested in her, Carolyn is determined to discover the truth about Jason's relationship with her mother, Liz.

EPISODE 5
Carolyn and Roger meet Barnabas and are struck by his resemblance to the old portrait. The two men drink together and discuss business.

EPISODE 6
An angry Burke warns Jason that Willie had certainly better be gone from Collinwood. Meanwhile a calf has been found dead, drained of all its blood; and then Willie, looking pale, appears at Collinwood. Jason discovers blood stains on Willie's sleeve.

EPISODE 7
Willie, growing weaker, gives vague answers to Jason's questions and after apologizing to Liz, faints at the sight of the portrait. Jason discovers a strange wound on Willie's arm, which he won't—or can't—explain.

EPISODE 8
Willie reveals to Vicki his dread of darkness. Ill and delirious, he wants to leave Collinwood. At nightfall, he hears a strange call. Looking at the portrait, he breaks away from Jason, races to the cemetery and enters the mausoleum.

EPISODE 9
Barnabas sees Jason looking for Willie in the mausoleum. When, later, Jason meets Barnabas, he recognizes him from the old portrait. Barnabas assures Jason that the jewels are hidden from grave robbers. He tries to persuade Liz and Roger to let him live in the Old House.

EPISODE 10
Liz tells Roger to order Willie out of Collinwood. The sheriff reveals that more dead animals have been found at the farm, drained of blood. And the doctor explains that Willie's illness is due to loss of blood. In fitful sleep, Willie moans that he can't return to the graveyard.

EPISODE 11
Liz permits Barnabas to move into the Old House. Willie, after apologizing to Vicki and attempting to speak to Liz, moves in with Barnabas.

EPISODE 12
Barnabas meets Maggie as she is closing the coffee shop for the night. She is clearly attracted to hi, but reveals to Joe Haskall that Barnabas fills her with an odd and eerie feeling. Barnabas will see more of Maggie. He order Willie to start his night-time task.

EPISODE 13
When Maggie comes to her cottage, she finds Barnabas waiting for her. And he commissions Sam, Maggie's father, to paint his portrait—working at the Old House, at night. Sam agrees. At sunrise, he is ushered back to his cottage by Willie.

EPISODE 14
Vicki reveals to Liza that Willie is now working for Barnabas at the Old House, and she is disturbed by the news. David, too, is disturbed since the portrait of Josette Collins is missing. He sneaks into the Old House, looking for it, when the door suddenly swings shut, effectively locked him within.

EPISODE 15 THROUGH 17
Missing plotlines

EPISODE 18
In the morning when Sam awakens Maggie, she feels strangely ill and collapses. That night, while Sam is working on the portrait, Barnabas slips out into the night. Maggie, at home alone, gets out of bed and obeys a strange compulsion to open her bedroom windows.

EPISODE 19
Jason advises Liz that someday she is going to have to explain his continued presence at Collinwood. Carolyn is growing suspicious about their relationship and learns that traces of her dead father are locked in the basement room, the key to which only her mother has.

EPISODE 20
There are some puncture wounds on Maggie's neck. Dr. Woodard tells Joe that her illness is due to blood loss. When Sam tells Burke and Vicki about Maggie's strange illness, Vicki recognizes the very symptoms that Willie suffered. Sam rushes home to find that Maggie is missing.

EPISODE 21
Vicki stands lone vigil at the cottage while Sam, Joe and Burke search for Maggie. Phoning anonymously, Willie informs Vicki that Maggie is at the cemetery. Burke discovers strange wounds on Maggie's neck. And Barnabas finds out about Willie's betrayal.

EPISODE 22
Dr. Woodard orders an immediate transfusion for Maggie and places her under 24-hour vigil, insisting that her window be locked. Sam is awakened by howling dogs and is just in time to restrain Maggie from leaving through the window.

EPISODE 23
Maggie can't remember anything. She can't explain that wounds on her neck. She tells Joe that she wants to break up with him. That night, with Vicki standing vigil, a shadowy figure is stirring outside Maggie's window. And Maggie, suddenly strong, insists on going out.

EPISODE 24
In the great drawing room of Collinwood, Barnabas describes to Carolyn and Vicki what life was like living there 100 years ago. Vicki begins asking searching questions, but is interrupted as Jason urges him to send Willie away.

EPISODE 25
Barnabas warns Willie not to see Jason. At night, while Vicki is standing vigil over Maggie, someone is trying to break into the cottage. Terrified, she phones Burke. When she returns, Maggie's room is locked, and the wolves are howling.

EPISODE 26
Maggie's wounds are now larger and she is at death's door. Dr. Woodard rushes her to the hospital and leaves strict orders that she is never to be left alone. When she appears dead, her nurse runs for help and returns to find that Maggie has vanished.

EPISODE 27
Suspecting Willie, Burke and Joe rush to the Old House, but Barnabas tells them that he is not there. When they leave, Maggie steps out of the shadows. Triumphantly, Barnabas tells Maggie that she is now Josette Collins and that he will resume their love affair—in marriage.

EPISODE 28
The sheriff questions Vicki, Burke and Jason. Willie rejects Jason's warnings to leave. Meanwhile, Dr. Woodard—unable to explain the wounds on Maggie's neck—fears she may be dead.

EPISODE 29
Carolyn and Vicki tell Liz how beautifully Barnabas has redecorated the Old House, particularly the upstairs room where they found Josette's portrait. That night, at dinner, Barnabas greets a lovely woman who seems to be Josette.

EPISODE 30
Maggie, in a trance, believes that she actually is Josette Collins. Barnabas hastily escorts her upstairs when Sam and Joe come calling unexpectedly. And when they leave, Barnabas comes back upstairs, where Willie has been guarding her, and closes in on Maggie.

EPISODE 31
When Liz tells David that they've found Josette's portrait, he disobeys orders and goes to the Old House. Barnabas firmly escorts him home and urges Roger to keep him away, but the boy sneaks back and comes fact-to-face with Maggie.

EPISODE 32
David believes Maggie is Josette. Barnabas, troubled, questions him but learns nothing. The sheriff informs Barnabas that the search for Maggie may have to end since she might be dead. David confesses to Vicki that he has seen Josette.

EPISODE 33
Roger confronts Liz with the charge that Jason is blackmailing her regarding the basement room. Meanwhile, Dr. Woodard informs Burke that he is turning Maggie's blood sample over to a woman specialist, Dr. Julia Hoffma. But the sample is stolen from his office.

EPISODE 34
Dr. Woodard informs Jason that the blood sample has been stolen. Jason can't find Willie and begins asking Barnabas some embarrassing questions, particularly about the Barnabas-Willie relationship. Back at Collinwood, Jason dares proposing marriage to Liz.

EPISODES 36-36
Storylines are missing

EPISODE 37
When Carolyn learns of her mother's coming marriage, she is convinced that Jason has some sort of strange "hold" on Liz. She is now determined to get into the basement room, and Jason surprisingly agrees to help her get the key, which Liz wears on a chain around her neck.

EPISODE 38
The sheriff tells Sam that Maggie may have been kidnapped, but there are no clues. Willie tries to convince her that she is Josette. When she slips out of the Old House, Barnabas goes rushing after her. Sam sees her outside the cottage window, but she disappears.

EPISODE 39
When Maggie sees Sam's pipe, she realizes she is not Josette. But Barnabas puts her in an adjoining coffin and Willie attempts to hypnotize her into believing she is Josette. She tries to escape, but is hopelessly trapped.

EPISODE 40
Jason warns Liz that Carolyn, Vicki and Roger are plotting to enter the basement room. He fixes it up and promises them he'll get the key. But Liz escorts them to the room. They find nothing. In triumph, Jason tells Liz to announce their marriage.

EPISODE 41
As a precaution, Maggie pretends to be Josette and Barnabas tells her the wedding will be tonight. Willie is still trying to hypnotize her, but she warns him that she'll kill Barnabas. Willie takes her to the coffin where Barnabas is sleeping. Just as she is set to kill, he opens his eyes.

EPISODE 42
In a rage, Barnabas tries to strangle Maggie, but Willie intercedes. And Vicki suddenly comes to the Old House. She's intrigued with the music box that Willie finds so helpful for hypnotizing. He promises to help Maggie, and Barnabas turns his attentions toward Vicki.

EPISODE 43
Missing storyline

EPISODE 44
Maggie is completely frustrated when her effort to get some word to her father proves futile. Barnabas is pressing her to marry him.

EPISODE 45
Carolyn is troubled about her mother's coming marriage to Jason, but he is gloating and even announces to Willie that he will soon be the master of Collinwood. And when he announces the wedding date to Carolyn, she announces that she'll wed Buzz at the same time.

EPISODE 46
While delivering the portrait to Barnabas, Sam tells him that the authorities have given up the search for Maggie. She is presumed dead. Barnabas now strongly urges Maggie to become Josette, and be his bride. Outside the basement, Maggie hearts a girl, singing.

EPISODE 47
Maggies tries vainly to speak to the strange girl, Sarah. David meets the girl; they talk and play together. She disappears and Willie promises he will be on the lookout for her. She returns to Maggie's "cell." Meantime, Carolyn advises Liz that she will definitely marry Buzz.

EPISODE 48
Concerned that Carolyn will marry Buzz, Liz asks Jason to stop her. He can't persuade Carolyn, but he offers Buzz a bribe, which he refuses.

EPISODE 49
Maggie is alone, calling Sarah. She appears, they sing and talk, and then the girl disappears again. Barnabas fears that Maggie has gone mad and tells Willie she will have to be disposed of. Willie tries to convince her that she has no secret friend, but Maggie finds Sarah's doll.

EPISODE 50
Carolyn feels that Liz has not remained loyal to the memory of her father. Jason advises Liz to give up on Carolyn. She says she loves her daughter, otherwise she'd tell her the truth. That night, sobbing, Liz confesses to Carolyn that she murdered Paul Stoddard.

EPISODE 51
Maggie escapes and before Barnabas can drag her back, Sam appears. She goes into shock. Sam, Joe and Dr. Woodard decide to pretend that Maggie is dead, and when this news is conveyed to Barnabas, he believes it.

EPISODE 52
Missing storyline.

EPISODE 53
Liz asks Vicki to be her legal witness at the wedding, and, reluctantly, she agrees. Vicki tells Carolyn that Maggie is dead and when Carolyn sees Joe—who pretends to be grief stricken—she decides to call her wedding off. Vicki can't persuade Liz to tell Carolyn the truth.

EPISODE 54

Carolyn and Vicki decide to do something about all the strange events that have been occurring. Vicki will go to Sam, Carolyn will go to Joe. Neither man can bring himself to confess that Maggie is alive. Later, the mere sight of Jason rekindles Carolyn's urge to get revenge on her mother.

EPISODE 55

When Roger informs Barnabas that Liz is going to marry Jason and that the property might be sold, Barnabas decides to speak to Jason. Meantime, Willie encounters Sarah who vaguely indicates that she lives in the Old House. Then she disappears. Barnabas and Jason threaten each other.

EPISODE 56

Sam decides to visit Maggie at the hospital, but Dr. Woodard tries to dissuade him—since Maggie is now under Julia's care. Sam insists. At the hospital, Julia is cold and distant, but agrees to let Sam see Maggie. She firmly advises Dr. Woodard that, in the future, she alone will decide who's to see Maggie.

EPISODE 57

Liz dreams that she jumps to her death off Widow's Hill. In the morning, she passively agrees to Jason's suggestion that they have a formal wedding. Mrs. Johnson finds Liz atop Widow's Hill, the brooding peak from which, according to legend, distraught Widow's leap to their death.

EPISODE 58

Liz is at the edge of Widow's Hill, when Barnabas grabs her from behind. He suspects that she was going to jump. He warns Vicki to keep an eye on her. Burke wants Vicki to quit her job, but she tells him that Liz is now suicidal and that she can't quit at this time. David sees Liz forlornly reading the family book, with its records of family suicides.

EPISODE 59

Roger is informed by family lawyer Richard Garner, that Liz has suddenly put her will in order. Liz says an oblique goodbye to David and Carolyn. When a terribly worried Vicki rushes to Liz's room, she finds it empty. Liz has inscribed her name in the family bible, adding the date of her death. She appears on Widow's Hill.

EPISODE 60

Vicki races to Widow's Hill and prevents Liz from killing herself. She decides she will go through with the wedding, but advises Jason that theirs will never be a real marriage. Burke now has some information about Jason's past, and when he confronts Jason with it, Jason merely invites him to the wedding.

EPISODE 61

Carolyn now prepares to take drastic action to prevent her mother from marrying Jason, but Liz is going ahead with the marriage.

EPISODE 62

In the middle of the wedding ceremony, Liz suddenly confesses that Jason is an accomplice in the murder of her husband, Paul Stoddard.

EPISODE 63

Digging in the crypt-like cellar of Collinwood, the sheriff discovers an old metal trunk.

EPISODE 64

When the long-buried trunk turns out to be empty, Liz realizes that her husband might still be alive.

EPISODE 65

Jason tries a little blackmail after overhearing the ominous plans that Barnabas has for Vicki.

EPISODE 66

Jason foolishly refuses to heed Willie's warning after discovering Barnabas' coffin in the Old House.

EPISODE 67

Maggie, still considered to be dead by the townspeople (but hidden away), remembers a frightening room of the Old House, from which she tried to escape.

An aged Barnabas Collins (Jonathan Frid) with Kathryn Leigh Scott.

Laura Parker

EPISODE 68
Having disposed of Jason, Barnabas plans a costume party and decides who will be the next occupant of the room of his 18th Century sweetheart, Josette.

EPISODE 69
Barnabas pays a call to Collinwood and invites Vicki to his home to select the costume she will wear to his party.

EPISODE 70
Barnabas wickedly rounds out his plan when he invites Burke, Vicki's fiance, to come to his costume party too.

EPISODE 71
Someone proposes a seance in order to contact the ghost that Liz suspects is present at the home of Barnabas.

EPISODE 72
In the trance during the seance, Vicki relives Josette's flight from a terrifying assailant.

EPISODE 73
Vicki is entranced by the music box that Barnabas has given her, while Maggie remembers something that terrifies her.

EPISODE 74
When Julia takes Maggie to the cemetery, Vicki thinks she recognizes a familiar face near Josette's grave.

EPISODE 75
Julia is now convinced that Maggie's amnesia is the result of an "unearthly" experience.

EPISODE 76
When a sudden storm arises, Barnabas invites Vicki to spend the night in his home.

EPISODE 77
Sleeping in the room of long-dead Josette, Vicki hears a child's voice chanting an eerie song.

EPISODE 78
Liz, believing that Julia is only a historian, agrees to cooperate with her.

EPISODE 79
After questioning young David about his mysterious, ghost-like playmate, Julia discovers the terrifying secret about Barnabas.

EPISODE 80
Julia breaks into Barnabas' home and makes her way down to the coffin room.

EPISODE 81
Vicki confides to Barnabas that his music box has had a strange effect on her.

EPISODE 82
Julia is now aware of the truth about Barnabas and offers him a starling proposition.

EPISODE 83
Barnabas distrusts Julia, but, trapped, he accepts her proposition and retains his quiet suspicions about her.

EPISODE 84
Keeping her end of of the quixotic agreement with Barnabas, Julia hypnotizes Maggie into keeping a secret.

EPISODE 85
Although Maggie's amnesia is cured by Julia, the terrifying experience with Barnabas remains a blank to her.

EPISODE 86
Barnabas and Julia seal their strange pact, each aware that others may be caught in the widening web of intrigue.

EPISODE 87
Maggie is reunited with her boyfriend, Joe Haskall, while Barnabas pursues his sinister plans for Maggie.

EPISODE 88
When Maggie's life is in jeopardy, young Sarah suddenly appears—out of thin air.

EPISODE 89
Carolyn has a terrible premonition of doom at the very same time that Maggie remembers a coffin that was not in a dream.

EPISODE 90
Aware that Barnabas is a vampire, Julia warns Vicki that her relationship with him could have terrible consequences.

EPISODE 91
Vicki dreams that someone enters her bedroom during the night. Later, she is unprepared to answer the crucial question posed by her fiance, Burke.

EPISODE 92
Storyline missing.

EPISODE 93
Vicki decides to marry Burke. Despite Julia's warnings, Barnabas will get revenge on Burke, who bears a strong resemblance to Jeremiah Collins, his long-dead enemy.

EPISODE 94
Burke wants the truth and questions both Dr. Woodard and Maggie. He returns to Vicki who, again, has been drawn to the haunting music box with its weird grip on her.

EPISODE 95
Blocked by Willie from seeing Barnabas, Burke now asks Vicki to keep away from Barnabas. Julia warns Willie to keep away from Burke; meantime she gets permission to take care of David.

EPISODE 96
Barnabas fears he will not get at Burke, but Julia assures him she will handle Burke. At the cemetery, Sarah leads David into the mausoleum and into the secret chamber.

EPISODE 97
Storyline missing.

EPISODE 98
Despite the danger, Maggie insists on returning to Collinsport. Vicki, Sam and Joe wants David to help them find Sarah as the key to the mystery. Vicki warns Burke that she will end their engagement if he does not stop his investigation of Barnabas.

EPISODE 99
David is not really helping in the search for Sarah. Maggie discovers Sarah's doll, which was left at the cottage. Sam suspects Julia and questions her about her relationship with Barnabas.

EPISODE 100
Vicki forces Burke to apologize to Barnabas, who is now convinced that Sarah has come back to expose him. Now Julia also joins the search for the child, and tells Barnabas that she has definitely been at the Old House.

EPISODE 101
In the cemetery, Sarah vanishes from David. Searching for her in the secret vault of the mausoleum, David hides when Barnabas and Willie enter.

EPISODE 102
David is trapped in the mausoleum. While Joe and Carolyn search for David, Barnabas races to Collinwood to comfort Vicki.

EPISODE 103
Vicki is saved when Joe and Carolyn return, but Barnabas now learns that David had been sent out to find Sarah. Now he knows where David is and that he must get to him before the sheriff does.

EPISODE 104
In a frantic search for David, Joe and Roger impulsively go to the cemetery. They leave the mausoleum just as David, now exhausted, awakens and vainly calls out to them.

EPISODE 105
When he learns that Sarah has revealed important secrets to David, Barnabas decides to kill the boy. Danger mounts when Dr. Woodard advises that laboratory tests indicate that Sarah's doll is 160 years old.

EPISODE 106
Sarah appears at the mausoleum, leads David to the door, then vanishes. David races out, and into the arms of Barnabas.

EPISODE 107
Burke rescues David from Barnabas, but Vicki keeps trusting Barnabas. David realizes he's in danger, but he can't tell Roger the truth.

EPISODE 108
Sam and Joe search the mausoleum and find proof that Sarah is a ghost. Both Julia and Barnabas realize that Sam and Joe know the truth.

EPISODE 109
Julia forces Barnabas to promise that he will not murder David—at least not tonight. Barnabas changes his mind, when Sarah suddenly appears, to Barnabas' horror. Dr. Woodard questions David, then firmly announces to Julia that he is taking Maggie out of her care.

EPISODE 110
Dr. Woodard decides to pretend publicly that Maggie's memory is returning. Barnabas is troubled by the news.

EPISODE 111
David confides to Burke that he is afraid of Barnabas. Vicki is annoyed at Burke's suspicions. Barnabas asks Julia to get rid of Maggie at once.

EPISODE 112
Sensing danger, Sarah suddenly appears in Maggie's room, but vanishes when Sam comes in. Sam assures Maggie that the cottage is surrounded by the police, while Barnabas, alone starts out into the night.

EPISODE 113
Creeping through the woods, Barnabas hears Sarah's music. Willie is determined to stop Barnabas from murdering Maggie.

EPISODE 114
Barnabas and Julia are stunned when the sheriff informs them that Willie has broken into Maggie's cottage. Barnabas does not consider Willie a threat, but he is determined to do something about David.

EPISODE 115
Vicki is shocked to learn that Willie is the madman everyone has been looking for. She's worried about David and his terrible fear of Barnabas. Julia begins pressing Vicki to learn if David has revealed anything to her.

EPISODE 116
Concerned over David, Liz and Vicki are pleased when Barnabas offers to speak with the boy in private. And after the talk, David is more frightened than ever. In a dream, Sarah appears to David and reveals the truth about her death.

EPISODE 117

When Barnabas learns that Willie is recovering, though still in a coma, he decides to murder him. But he feels David's the greater threat. Julia goes to David and unveils her medallion, the one she used to hypnotize Maggie.

EPISODE 118

David sneaks out to go searching for Sarah. Burke interrupts them in the woods, Sarah vanishes and David reveals to Burke that Sarah is a ghost. That night, Sarah returns to David, reveals Willie's innocence and warns him to stay away from the Old House.

EPISODE 119

To convince the sheriff of Willie's guilt, Barnabas plants Maggie's ring in Willie's hospital room. He's rallying from his coma. Barnabas orders Julia to kill Willie.

EPISODE 120

The sheriff questions Willie and considers him insane—much to the delight of Barnabas.

EPISODE 121

Despite Sarah's warning, David sneaks into the Old House, but Julia sends him home. Barnabas decides he won't have to kill David, but will only have to firmly establish David's reputation as an incurable liar. And so that night a giant bat attacks David in his room.

EPISODE 122

While calming David with a sedative, Dr. Woodard begins wondering about the supernatural—specifically Sarah's visitations. Sarah appears and offers David a toy soldier, assuring him it will provide protection.

EPISODE 123

David steals Liz' key to the basement room. He shows Vicki his toy soldier and she, in turn, shows it to Liz and Roger. David sneaks into the Old House, where Barnabas is waiting for him.

EPISODE 124

David discovers an open coffin in the basement, but Julia saves him from Barnabas. Both Dr. Woodard and Burke now believe David and insist on inspecting the basement room. Barnabas agrees, but they find nothing.

EPISODE 125

Breaking his promise to Sarah, David tells Burke and Dr. Woodard about the secret room in the mausoleum. Roger is now concerned over David's mental state and feels that Vicki's coming marriage to Burke is poorly timed. He refuses permission to David to lead Dr. Woodard and Burke to the secret room of the mausoleum.

EPISODE 126

Liz has a psychiatrist examine David, and when Dr. Woodard hears the report (particularly about Barnabas' fangs), he goes to the mausoleum, where he finds Sarah. Liz tells Burke that the property he'd like to buy won't be legally available for five years.

EPISODE 127

Sarah opens the secret vault for Dr. Woodard. He finds the coffin, but Sarah vanishes when he asks about Barnabas. Curious about the Collins family, Dr. Woodard begins searching the books in the library—to Julia's annoyance.

EPISODE 128

Dr. Woodard assures David that he believes him, then confronts Barnabas with the news that he has met Barnabas' sister, Sarah. Burke wants to set the wedding date, but Vicki is reluctant to leave Collinwood at this time.

EPISODE 129

Barnabas tells Julia of Dr. Woodard's suspicions and urges her to destroy her notes. At the window, Dr. Woodard overhears Julia assure Barnabas that her notes are safely locked in a strong box in her room. Liz offers to open Collinwood's west wing to Burke and Vicki so that they can marry soon, but Burke wants them to leave Collinwood.

Jonathan Frid with Joan Bennett

EPISODE 130
Dr. Woodard steals Julia's notes. Julia openly admits to Barnabas that she cares for him. Together they go to the main house and discover Liz and Roger arguing about opening the west wing for Burke and Vicki.

EPISODE 131
Barnabas kills Dr. Woodard and with Julia's help, disguises the murder to look like a heart attack. Sam and the sheriff discover the dead doctor.

EPISODE 132
Sam and Burke doubt the sheriff's report that Dr. Woodard died a natural death. Meantime, Julia—pretending grief—is consoled by Vicki.

EPISODE 133
Vicki doesn't want to leave Collinwood at this time, and her fiance, Burke, does not want her to move into the west wing. Julia resents Burke's interest in Vicki.

EPISODE 134
Sarah informs David that something dreadful is about to happen. David is deeply troubled when he learns that Burke must go to Brazil.

EPISODE 135
Liz gives Vicki the terrible news of a plane crash in Brazil, and that Burke will probably never return. But Barnabas reassures Vicki, then informs Julia that Vicki will be the next Josette. Julia is jealous.

EPISODE 136
Anticipating Burke's return, Vicki accepts Barnabas' offer to help restore the west wing. Julia, inflamed with jealousy, tries to kill Vicki.

EPISODE 137
Barnabas urges Julia to expedite her experiments: he is responding under them, and now feels ready to watch the sunrise—with Vicki. Julia hypnotizes Vicki and leads her to Barnabas in his coffin. Later, she remembers nothing.

EPISODE 138
David warns Carolyn that she is in danger and gives her Sarah's toy soldier for protection. Carolyn persuades Liz that David must be sent away, when Sarah appears to her. Barnabas insists on massive treatments, and turns into a withered old man.

EPISODE 139
Since Barnabas now needs a victim as an antidote, Julia suggests Vicki. Barnabas refuses. Carolyn confesses to Joe that he has seen Sarah. That night, Barnabas hovers over Vicki's bed, but disappears when Carolyn enters.

EPISODE 140
Julia offers her neck to Barnabas, but he declines. Trying to mislead Carolyn, David claims he has been telling lies, but Carolyn now wants to see the Old House for herself. She sneaks into the coffin room, and is surprised by Barnabas—who closes in on her.

EPISODE 141
Carolyn, in a trance, regains consciousness in Josette's room. She is completely under Barnabas' spell. Now a young man again, Barnabas informs Julia that she will no longer be needed. He orders Carolyn to help him win Vicki, also to help him discredit David.

EPISODE 142
Carolyn informs Julia that David is no longer a threat, also that she will take care of Vicki. Jealous of Carolyn, Julia hypnotizes Vicki and tells her that Barnabas is going to make her his bride. Carolyn suspects Julia.

EPISODE 143
Storyline missing.

EPISODE 144
Liz and Roger ask Vicki to accompany David on a trip to Boston. Julia shows Vicki, who is hypnotized, the coffin that Barnabas plans for her to occupy once he has killed her. Maggie returns and is struck by the odd change in Carolyn.

EPISODE 145
Carolyn sneaks into Julia's room, looking for the secret notes of her experiments. Julia bursts in on her and now realizes that Barnabas wants her dead. Maggie returns and is struck by the odd change in Carolyn.

EPISODE 146
Carolyn suspects that Julia will use the daylight hours to kill Barnabas. Julia warns Barnabas that as long as she has her notebook, Barnabas would be signing his own death warrant by murdering her. Julia hides her notebook in the foyer block, while Barnabas moves his coffin to another room.

EPISODE 147
Realizing that Carolyn is hot on the trail of the notebook, Julia takes it into town. She leaves it with Tony Peterson, a lawyer, now annoyed with the Collins family. Carolyn has followed Julia into town.

EPISODE 148
Carolyn tells Barnabas that Julia's notebook is hidden and Barnabas decides on tactics intended to drive Julia insane.

EPISODE 149
Julia distinctly hears the voice of Dr. Woodard and is terrified. On a date with Tony, Carolyn pries for information about Julia, who is now prepared to fight Barnabas.

EPISODE 150
Julia is desperate to contact Sarah. She rushes to the cemetery and finally finds Sarah at the mausoleum. Julia asks Sarah who to trust, but Sarah is vague in her answers.

EPISODE 151
Julia, trapped in the mausoleum, manages to escape. She races to Collinwood and receives a telephone call from Dr. Woodard, informing her that she is going to die.

EPISODE 152
Barnabas urges Carolyn to steal Tony's keys, break into his office and get Julia's notebook—tonight. Barnabas plans to put an end to her quickly. Tony discovers Carolyn pilfering his keys.

EPISODE 153
Tony, confused, doesn't know whether to believe Carolyn or Julia. Sarah abruptly leaves David and rushes to the Old House, entering just as Barnabas is strangling Julia. And for the first time, Sarah now appears before Barnabas.

EPISODE 154
Liz informs Vicki that Burke's plane has been found, but there are no signs of him. Sarah confesses to David that "the dead" are going to destroy somebody at Collinwood. Julia assures Liz and Vicki that David is telling the truth.

EPISODE 155
Determined that contact with Sarah be made, Liz, Roger, Vicki and Carolyn hold a seance. Sarah speaks—through Vicki. When the lights go on, Vicki is missing, though the windows and doors are still shut.

EPISODE 156
Vicki races through the woods to the Old House, which suddenly looks new. Vicki realizes that he has been mysteriously transported back through time to 1795; back to the world of the Collins family ancestors—the world of Barnabas, his younger sister Sarah, his parents, family and friends.

EPISODE 157
Vicki awakens from sleep discovering that the year is 1795, and the woman beside her is Abigail Collins—the elder sister of Joshua Collins (Barnabas' father). Vicki runs out and races into the arms of a man who looks exactly like Burke. It is Jeremiah Collins. He promises to help Vicki and gets Joshua to hire her as the governess.

EPISODE 158
Barnabas is troubled because he knows Josette's boat is overdue. He wants to go to the boatyards, but Angelique, the Collins' maidservant, brings news that Countess Natalie's carriage is mired down the road. Joshua sends Barnabas to help. Joshua and Natalie instinctively dislike each other, but the Countess is a guest in the home and Joshua is polite.

EPISODE 159
Josette finally arrives and flies into Barnabas' waiting arms. Angelique is jealous, and has stolen a toy soldier Barnabas had as a child. Now she tightens a handkerchief around its neck and Barnabas himself begins to choke.

EPISODE 160
The doctor can find nothing wrong with Barnabas. Deeply concerned, Jeremiah asks Angelique to help lest Barnabas die. Horrified, Angelique runs to her room and unties the handkerchief from the neck of the toy soldier.

EPISODE 161
Realizing she needs an accomplice, Angelique brews a poisonous elixir and gives it to Ben Stokes, making him her slave. Joshua strongly dislikes Ben. Millicent Collins arrives, ready for the family-arranged marriage to Jeremiah.

EPISODE 162
Angelique plans to make Josette fall in love with Jeremiah. She proves her witchcraft powers to Ben. Jeremiah resents the wedding, resents the domineering ways of his brother Joshua. Vicki reassures Jeremiah, reminding him that Millicent died a spinster. Ben serves Angelique's brew to Jeremiah and steals his ring.

EPISODE 163
Ben is so pleased that Barnabas plans to take over his indenture, that he almost tells him the truth about Angelique. But he is firmly under her spell. Angelique works her powers on Josette, who finds herself confessing to Jeremiah that she loves him.

EPISODE 164
Angelique decides to make Jeremiah fall in love with Josette. She administers her potion to him. Josette tries to persuade Natalie to go on an expedition with Barnabas. Later, Natalie sees Jeremiah and Josette meet.

EPISODE 165
Natalie tells Andre that a witch is conspiring to prevent the marriage of his daughter, Josette, to Barnabas. Naomi is shocked when Natalie implies that Vicki may be a witch. Andre warns Jeremiah never to see Josette alone.

EPISODE 166
Nathan discovers that Millicent Collins is an heiress and begins to pursue her. Angelique realizes she is too powerless to stop the evil she has set in motion. Jeremiah informs Josette that he will leave Collinsport tonight. On his hand is the brand that symbolizes evil. And on Josette's hand too.

EPISODE 167
Angelique knows she must prevent Jeremiah from leaving. She turns Joshua into a black cat. Now Jeremiah must remain and be the master of the household. Josettes comes out of her spell.

EPISODE 168
Natalie knows that witchcraft is responsible for Joshua's disappearance. She blames Vicki. Vicki rearranges Natalie's tarot cards so that Natalie persuades Barnabas to marry Josette at once—if Josette is willing.

EPISODE 169
Josette and Barnabas agree on an immediate wedding. Angelique casts a spell on Josette, and she and her luggage disappear.

EPISODE 170
Jermiah's luggage is gone. Gun in hand, Barnabas races out to search for Josette. Hearing a voice, Barnabas shoots at a shadowy figure and later finds Josette's mud-strained wedding gown. Angelique is now satisfied that she has poisoned Barnabas against Josette.

EPISODE 171
Natalie urges Naomi to question Vicki. Abigail searches Vicki's room when, suddenly, the black cat turns back into Joshua. He is furious that they did not prevent Josette's and Jeremiah's marriage. Abigail and Natalie find a charm bracelet among Vicki's clothes and realize that she is a witch.

EPISODE 172
The newlyweds, Josette and Jeremiah, prepare for bed. The brand on Josette's hand wears off—the spell is ended. Tearfully, Josette asks to be taken back to Barnabas. Joshua decides to send for a witch hunter. Josette and Jeremiah return. The brand is now gone from his hand too. Both realize what they have done.

EPISODE 173
Josette begs her father to prevent the duel between Barnabas and Jeremiah. Angelique realizes she must protect Barnabas. She casts a spell on Josette. In the duel, Barnabas shoots and Josette races to her fallen husband, and screams at Barnabas for wounding the only man she has ever loved.

EPISODE 174
Nathan warns Vicki about the witch hunt. Reverand Trask, the witch hunting minister, fails to extract a confession from Vicki. He carries her, gagged, into the woods—leaving her tied to a tree, where she can spend the night alone, with an opportunity to recant.

EPISODE 175
Nathan and Barnabas find Vicki and bring her back, hiding her in an empty room. Meantime, Angelique sets the tree afire. In the morning, Trask finds the tree has burned. He realizes Vicki was a witch.

EPISODE 176
Angelique advises Trask to search Collinwood in his witch-hunt. She knows that Nathan is there, smuggling food to Vicki. Trask forbids Joshua from moving into Collinwood until the evil spirits are driven out. Joshua discovers Nathan, but Vicki escapes.

EPISODE 177
Trask discovers that Josette has been bewitched and insists on exorcising the devil from her. Barnabas admits to Angelique his love for Josette. Wounded, she decides to use Sarah to get revenge on Barnabas, and clutches one of her dolls.

EPISODE 178
Sarah falls mysteriously ill and wants only Vicki. Naomi sees Vicki's tender treatment of Sarah and concludes that Vicki is not a witch. Ben is furious with Angelique and tries to kill her. She informs Barnabas that she will cure Sarah if he will marry her. He promises. Angelique gives him a tea for Sarah and she recovers.

EPISODE 179
Josette fears that Jeremiah will die. Barnabas tells Naomi he will marry Angelique. And Angelique tells Josette that Barnabas does not forgive her. Josette wants to die. She awakens and sees the figure of Jeremiah; she races to the room to find he has just died.

EPISODE 180
Barnabas informs Joshua that he will marry Angelique. Josette hears the voice of Jeremiah summoning her to his side. She goes out into the night, followed by Naomi. A hand reaches out from Jeremiah's grave. Josette screams as Naomi comes running to her.

EPISODE 181
Jeremiah's ghost appears to Josette and she realizes that he is urging her to commit suicide. Natalie assigns Angelique to sleep in the room with Josette. They move into Collinwood and find that the door to Jeremiah's room will not open. they hear, from inside the room, the ghostly laugh of a man.

Grayson Hall

EPISODE 182
Abigail confronts Angelique who later summons the ghost of Jeremiah. The ghost threatens Barnabas with haunting him forever if he should marry Josette. Barnabas, frightened, tells Jeremiah that he is going to marry Angelique.

EPISODE 183
Joshua disinherits Barnabas for insisting on marrying Angelique at once. In retaliation, Naomi—who owns the Old House—gives it to Barnabas. Angelique is alone in the Old House when the ghost of Jeremiah suddenly appears.

EPISODE 184
Angelique is in her wedding gown. In the mirror, her gown appears torn and bloodied. Barnabas now agrees to help Vicki, who, sobbing, tells him the truth about herself. He doubts her story. The ghost of Jeremiah steals Angelique away and pushes her into a grave.

EPISODE 185
Ben finds Angelique at Jeremiah's grave. She and Barnabas are married. Barnabas and Naomi are startled by still another display of the supernatural. Angelique finds a music box that Barnabas had bought for Josette. Jeremiah's ghost returns and Angelique demands to know who at Collinwood is summoning him.

EPISODE 186
Angelique decides she will have Abigail get Vicki. She commands Ben to steal a brooch from Abigail's room. Abigail catches him and he explains that the was sent there by the witch.

EPISODE 187
Angelique casts a spell on Vicki so that Sarah hears Vicki's voice calling her to the Old House. Sarah informs Vicki of a hiding place in the Old House—the attic. Now Sarah and Abigail suspect Vicki.

EPISODE 188
Storyline missing.

EPISODE 189
Barnabas now suspects that the witch is either Vicki or Angelique and extracts the correct identification from Ben.

EPISODE 190
Remembering all of Angelique's villainy, Barnabas decides to kill her. Angelique suspects Barnabas' plot.

EPISODE 191
Angelique warns Barnabas to let her live as a witch—or Josette will die. She conjures up a bat to watch Barnabas, who now plans to leave Collinwood with Josette.

EPISODE 192
Vicki, in jail awaiting trial as a witch, meets Peter Bradford, a young, budding lawyer who believes her story. Josette is ready to flee with Barnabas. They make their plans—as the bat looks on.

EPISODE 193
With Natalie and Josette away, Abigail asks Angelique to be her witness at the witch trial. Barnabas hangs Josette's portrait in the drawing room and Angelique is furious. Barnabas kills her, but before dying, Angelique puts a curse on him. The bat attacks him.

EPISODE 194
At the Old House, Ben discovers that Barnabas, after the attack, is still breathing. En route to Boston with Natalie, Josette instinctively knows that Barnabas is in trouble. She wants to return to Collinsport. Angelique revives, and prevents Barnabas from calling a doctor.

EPISODE 195
While ostensibly trying to cure Barnabas, Angelique notifies Naomi that Barnabas has gone on a trip. Josette returns, looking for him. She is aghast at the blood gashes on his neck and his delirium.

EPISODE 196
Convinced of witchcraft, Josette begs Vicki to lift the spell on Barnabas. Vicki pleads with Josette to leave Collinsport to avert her dreadful fate as recorded in the family album. Josette reads the family album and is stunned. She has just read about her own death.

EPISODE 197
Josette and Natalie agree that the family album is a hoax since it indicates that Barnabas moved to England. On his death bed, Barnabas makes Josette promise to wait for him to return. After his death, a bat crashes through the window. Joshua announces that it will be recorded that Barnabas moved to England.

EPISODE 198
Josette refuses to return to her native Martinique, knowing that Barnabas will be back. In order to prevent his living an eternal life among the walking dead, Angelique plans to break into the mausoleum and murder him.

EPISODE 199
At dusk, Barnabas arises from his coffin just as Angelique is about to murder him. Realizing that she is the witch, Barnabas murders Angelique. He discovers Ben in the mausoleum and a pledge is made that Ben will continue as Barnabas' servant. Barnabas regrets murdering Angelique, realizing the ghastly life he must now lead.

EPISODE 200
Josette is bitter and vows to kill the witch. With Peter's permission, Vicki leaves jail to steal the incriminating family album.

EPISODE 201
Sarah has made a gift for Josette, hoping it will bring Barnabas back. Eager to save Sarah from the destiny recorded in the family book, Vicki urges Naomi to keep Sarah home at all times. Sarah thinks she sees Barnabas outside and follows him through the graveyard.

EPISODE 202
Locked in the mausoleum, Sarah calls for Barnabas. On the boat docks, Barnabas sinks his fangs into the neck of Ruby Tate. She falls into the ocean and drowns. He returns to the mausoleum, frightening Sarah with his bloodied appearance.

EPISODE 203
Ben rescues Sarah and takes her home. She is drenched in the rain. Naomi and Millicent tend to the sick child. At dusk, Barnabas rises from his coffin to go to Sarah's room. Ben helps him to get to the dying girl. Sarah dies; the curse has started to work.

EPISODE 204
Barnabas feels that he killed Sarah. More than ever, he wants to die and begs Ben to drive a stake through his heart, to which he agrees.

EPISODE 205
Before dying, Barnabas wants to see Josette one last time. When Natalie discovers him in Josette's room, Barnabas immediately evaporates. Natalie warns Josette to flee for her life. At the mausoleum, Ben prepares to carry out the murder of Barnabas when the ghost of Angelique comes to prevent it.

EPISODE 206
Angelique leads Josette to the mausoleum, telling her that she will be reunited with Barnabas there. Barnabas warns her of the danger and urges her to leave. She hugs him and, suddenly, he notices her beautiful neck.

EPISODE 207
Not knowing that Nathan is married to Suky, Millicent agrees to marry him. Millicent wonders about Josette's story about seeing Barnabas. He fears if he sees Josette again, he will make her his.

EPISODE 208
Suky comes to Collinwood, posing as Nathan's sister. Josette will leave tomorrow, and Barnabas burst into her room for one final visit. When Josette falls into her arms, he can't resist...and bites her. Josette is doomed.

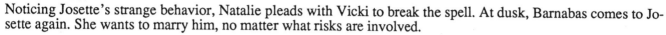

EPISODE 209
Noticing Josette's strange behavior, Natalie pleads with Vicki to break the spell. At dusk, Barnabas comes to Josette again. She wants to marry him, no matter what risks are involved.

EPISODE 210
At twilight, Josette can't control her urge to see Barnabas. He offers her one last chance for freedom. But she wants him. Joshua goes to the tomb where he buried Barnabas...and finds it empty.

EPISODE 211
Joshua tells Natalie that Barnabas' coffin is empty. Suky now insists on meeting Nathan in privacy at the Old House. Barnabas wants her to leave, but she discovers who he is and he kills her. When Nathan returns, she gasps the name, "Barnabas."

EPISODE 212
Joshua and Natalie fear that Josette will die tomorrow, exactly as recorded in the family book. Meanwhile, Millicent discovers that Suky was Nathan's wife, not his sister.

EPISODE 213
Angelique assures Ben that she will prevent Barnabas from marrying Josette. At Widow's Hill, Josette is terrified by Barnabas' ghastly appearance. Instead of joining him, she screams and leaps to her death.

EPISODE 214
With the death of Josette, Barnabas realizes Angelique's curse is at work and will destroy anybody who loves him. Millicent sees Barnabas and tells Ben that she needs Barnabas. Joshua decides to investigate the strange event.

EPISODE 215
Trask and Abigail set the date for Vicki's trial. When things go bad at the trial, Peter decides to question Ben about the witch.

EPISODE 216
Fearing Joshua, Ben refuses to testify at Vicki's trial. Joshua investigates and finds that Barnabas' coffin is not empty now.

EPISODE 217
Peter realizes he must bury the family book in the graveyard, lest it be used against Vicki. Barnabas is distraught at seeing Ben dig Josette's grave and decides he must destroy Ben.

EPISODE 218
Barnabas decides to use all the occult powers at his command to raise Josette from the dead. She comes to him, lifts the veil from her face and Barnabas shrinks back at her mangled countenance.

EPISODE 219
Against Ben's judgement, Ben's judgement, Barnabas realizes he must now kill Abigail. Trask relentlessly questions Daniel about Vicki. Frightened, the boy runs out into the night and discovers Abigail's body.

EPISODE 220
Storyline missing

EPISODE 221
At the witch trial, Trask accuses Vicki of murdering Abigail. Peter Persuades Nathan to testify in Vicki's defense. He agrees, but on the stand betrays Vicki.

EPISODE 222
In return for perjuring himself on the witness stand, Nathan reminds Trask to pay the reward which the reverence promised. Trask persuades Joshua to forgive Nathan. Naomi is furious and will testify at the trial.

EPISODE 223
Barnabas orders Ben to testify in Vicki's defense. Ben reveals that Angelique is the witch. Suddenly Angelique materializes in the courtroom. Only Ben knows that she is a ghost. Angelique condemns Vicki and the judge strikes Ben's testimony from the record.

EPISODE 224
Peter goes to the Old House to find Angelique. Ben insists that she is dead and digs up her coffin. Peter is convinced that Ben is a maniac. Peter urges Vicki to testify in her own defense, despite the risk.

EPISODE 225
Trask demands that Nathan testify again. Nathan testifies that Vicki bewitched him. Peter submits the Family History book as evidence. The judge finds Vicki guilty and sentences her to be hanged.

EPISODE 226
Barnabas vows to avenge the injustice. That night, alone in his room, Trask feels a disembodied hand grasp him by the throat.

EPISODE 227
Barnabas decides on the way he will kill Trask. At the shipyards, Barnabas attacks Maude and, inadvertently, drops his cane.

EPISODE 228
Barnabas sends Ben to find his cane. Later, Nathan sees Ben reporting to Barnabas, and realizes that Barnabas is the Collinsport strangler. Barnabas kills Maude and deposits her body in Trask's bed.

EPISODE 229
When Nathan discovers Maude's dead body in Trask's bed, the two men pledge to help each other. But the reverend's efforts to reconcile Nathan and Millicent are foiled by Naomi.

EPISODE 230
Barnabas extracts a written confession from Trask that Vicki is innocent. Then he orders Ben to seal up the reverend permanently in a brick tomb.

EPISODE 231
Nathan and Rex conspire against Millicent. Disguised as the Collinsport strangler, Rex attacks Millicent with Barnabas' cane. Peter shows Natalie Trask's written confession, then decides to go to Salem to see Trask.

EPISODE 232
Nathan "rescues" Millicent from the attack; she thinks Barnabas attacked her. Despite Naomi's warning, Millicent sneaks off to be with Nathan.

EPISODE 233
Nathan blackmails Joshua into consenting to his marrying Millicent. Joshua rushes to the Old House, slips into the basement room. Barnabas' coffin opens and Barnabas and Joshua are face to face.

EPISODE 234
Barnabas confesses to Joshua that he is the Collinsport strangler. Joshua pulls his pistol, but pauses when he hears Naomi upstairs. Joshua consents to Nathan's demands to marry Millicent. Joshua returns to the coffin room and shoots Barnabas through the heart.

EPISODE 235
Joshua is shocked to discover that bullets will not kill Barnabas. He now realizes that Angelique is the witch. He insists that Barnabas return to Collinwood where he can live in secret, hidden even from Naomi. Millicent announces that she will marry Nathan.

EPISODE 236
After the wedding, Nathan learns that Millicent will give her fortune to Daniel. Nathan devises a campaign designed to drive Millicent insane. Nathan realizes that Joshua is hiding Barnabas in Collinwood's tower room.

David Selby

EPISODE 237

Natalie tells Joshua about a good witch, Bathia, who can help them. Nathan sends Millicent to the tower room to investigate the place. Barnabas seizes her hand and sinks his fangs into her neck.

EPISODE 238

Joshua discovers Millicent, now insane, in his room. Bathia promises Joshua she will help Barnabas. But Barnabas lunges at Bathia and begins to strangle her.

EPISODE 239

Bathia insists that Barnabas be returned to the Old House where she can work on him in privacy. Nobody is to intrude. Naomi discovers Bathia in the Old House and Bathia goes up in flames.

EPISODE 240

Joshua tells Vicki that he knows she is innocent. Peter returns and, holding the jailer at gunpoint, leads Vicki from prison. An accidental gunblast wounds Vicki in the shoulder.

EPISODE 241

Peter and Vicki escape to the Old House, and Ben leads them to safety in the mausoleum. Daniel discovers Vicki and is pleased that she is free. In a dream, Vicki sees Nathan attempting to kill Daniel.

EPISODE 242

Nathan "hires" Noah to abduct and destroy Daniel, but Daniel escapes and runs to the mausoleum, where Vicki hides him in the secret room.

EPISODE 243

Huddled in the secret room, Vicki and Daniel await Peter's return. Daniel leaves to summon medical aid for Vicki and runs into the clutches of Noah. Noah begins strangling Daniel and Vicki shoots him. Peter discovers Noah's body and Nathan drags peter to jail.

EPISODE 244

Vicki wants to give herself up, but Naomi persuades her to wait until Joshua returns. Naomi threatens Nathan that she will have the police investigate Daniel's disappearance, but Nathan warns that he will expose Barnabas as the Collinsport strangler.

EPISODE 245

Naomi orders Ben to escort Daniel to safety in Reverend Bland's home. Millicent slips out into the night, with Naomi following her. Naomi sees Barnabas bite Millicent.

EPISODE 246

Naomi can't be consoled. She takes poison and leaves a note for Joshua. Then she goes to the tower room, tells Barnabas that she forgives him and collapses in his arms. Nathan takes Vicki to jail to collect the reward.

EPISODE 247

Barnabas is now more than ready to cooperate with Joshua in Joshua's plan to destroy him. But first Barnabas will take care of Nathan. Learning that Barnabas can be destroyed if a wooden stake is driven through his heart, Nathan sets a trap for him.

EPISODE 248

Nathan's trap fails and Barnabas kills him. Joshua finds a way to seal Barnabas in his tomb forever. Joshua fails to same Vicki. Peter comes to bid her farewell and Vicki is hung.

EPISODE 249

It is the seance in Collinwood in which Vicki disappeared and a strange woman in old style clothes appeared in her place. But then the woman disappears and Vicki is back at the table, having fainted. Back in 1795, the witch has been hung, but those assembled are shocked to see that she has changed her form into that of another woman. Back in the 20th Century, Barnabas revives Vicki. Julia Joffman announces that she is a doctor and volunteers to take care of Vicki. Barnabas is convinced that somehow Vicki was in 1795 and he fears that she knows his secret.

EPISODE 250
In a dream, Vicki sees Jeremiah Collins, who warns her that Barnabas wants her dead. Julia learns what Vicki remembers of her trip into the past and the record book confirms the existence of a Peter Bradford who was hung shortly after the witch was, having been charged with the murder of Noah. Vicki is inconsolable over the news that Peter just died almost 200 years ago. That night Barnabas attacks Vicki.

EPISODE 251
Vicki has purchased an old portrait, which turns out to be that of Angelique. Barnabas is horrified at this reminder of the horrors of his past. The vampire chooses to extend his control by biting Carolyn and making her his slave. But Barnabas doesn't know that Tony is looking in the window of the Old House when Carolyn becomes the victim of Barnabas. Tony thinks it is a young woman making love with her cousin, and is disgusted by the sight.

EPISODE 252
Barnabas attempts to burn the portrait of Angelique, but it cannot be destroyed. Professor Stokes sees the portrait and wants to buy it, but Roger refuses to allow Vicki to sell it. Roger is fascinated by the portrait and wants it for himself. Barnabas feels that he must gain mastery over Vicki. Julia begins to catch on when she finds the telltale mark of the vampire on Vicki's neck.

EPISODE 253
Vicki drams about Peter and needs to prove to herself that what happened to her in the past was real. She enlists the aid of Barnabas, as she feels that if she finds the secret room in the mausoleum, it† will prove that it wasn't all a dream.

EPISODE 254
Vicki is driving Barnabas with hr to the cemetery at Eagle Hill, when a man runs across the road in front of the car. Vicki recognizes him as Peter Bradford, her long lost lover from the past, and swerves the car to avoid hitting him, crashing into a tree in the process. Dr. Lang treats Barnabas, having determined that something about him is most odd. Barnabas awakens in the hospital room and is nervous about remaining. When he insists that he leave immediately, Dr. Land pulls back the curtain, exposing Barnabas to the sunlight. Barnabas screams.

EPISODE 255
Barnabas just screamed out of reflex. There is no pain from the sunlight. Dr. Lang guessed the truth about him and provided a cure, at least temporarily. But Barnabas is cynical and doesn't believe that it can be permanent.

EPISODE 256
Vicki is released from the hospital. The fang marks are gone from her neck and Carolyn is no longer under the spell of Barnabas, although she doesn't remember what she has recently done. Vicki and Julia go to the mausoleum to search for the secret room.

EPISODE 257
Just as he feared, Barnabas feels his vampire urges returning. Dr. Lang admits that his cure is not permanent, but he knows of a way to make it so.

EPISODE 258
Roger has become obsessed with the portrait of Angelique. He is even starting to act like his ancestor, Joshua, and sometimes calls his sister Naomi. Barnabas has been wooing Vicki, but she reveals that she can't marry him because she has found Jeff Clark, whom she believes is Peter Bradford.

EPISODE 259
Roger Collins has disappeared, something which is uncharacteristic of him as he never goes off without telling someone. Barnabas goes to Dr. Lang and the doctor reveals how he can be cured of vampirism once and for all, and get Vicki Winters as his bride—by acquiring the physical appearance of Jeff Clark, who is Dr. Lang's assistance.

EPISODE 260
Roger turns up at Dr. Lang's office, still under the thrall of Angelique's portrait. Barnabas and Julia arrive at the office just in time to prevent Roger from killing Dr. Lang. Roger comes to his senses and decides to get rid of the portrait by taking it to Professor Stokes. But the portrait suddenly turns blank and appears back at Collinwood.

EPISODE 261
Roger doesn't return to Collinwood at first, worrying his sister. When Roger does return it is with a new bridge at his arm, a woman named Cassandra who looks just like the woman in the portrait, except with darker hair. Everyone is shocked, particularly Barnabas.

EPISODE 262
Elizabeth is angry with Roger for doing this behind everyone's back and wants to know more about Cassandra. Barnabas knows that this is Angelique, who has returned because Barnabas is on the verge of being freed from her curse once and for all. Cassandra plays the innocent, but Barnabas is on his guard.

EPISODE 263
Cassandra sprains her ankle so that Roger cannot take her on their promised honeymoon trip. She visits Dr. Lang for treatment of her ankle and tries to kill him.

EPISODE 264
Dr. Lang reveals that, like Dr. Frankenstein, he has created a human body. He explains that he will transfer the lifeforce from Barnabas into that body. Barnabas is suspicious and wants the body to look like Jeff Clark. Meanwhile, Jeff Clark admits that he doesn't know who he really is or remember his past.

EPISODE 265
Cassandra uses her powers to force Tony Peterson to assist her evil scheme. As Angelique, she appears to Barnabas in a dream, promising that her curse of vampirism will return.

EPISODE 266
Cassandra meets Maggie Evans and immediately sees that she is the image of the long dead Josette. Cassandra starts her dream curse with Maggie, giving her the first round of a horrible dream that will pass from one to the other until they climax with Barnabas.

EPISODE 267
Dr. Lang is about to kill Jeff Clark by decapitation to give Jeff's face to his creation, but Barnabas has a change of heart and saves Jeff's life.

EPISODE 268
Barnabas wants Dr. Hoffman to hypnotize Jeff into forgetting about the experiment, but first Jeff tells Julia about Lang's plans. She decides to investigate Lang for herself.

EPISODE 269
Julia discovers the creation of Dr. Lang and vows to stop it. Barnabas and Lang prevent her from calling the police. Julia doesn't want Barnabas to go along with the experiment and Cassandra overhears them.

EPISODE 270
Cassandra sends Tony to steal Lang's medallion which protects him from witchcraft. Tony succeeds, but Barnabas and Lang discover that it's gone. Maggie tells Jeff her dream and then Jeff has the same one, only slightly more horrible than Maggie's was.

EPISODE 271
Dr. Lang needs a new assistance now that he cannot count on Jeff Clark. Willie Loomis seems the perfect choice and Barnabas convinces Julia to get him released from Windcliff, where he had been imprisoned for supposedly kidnapping Maggie Evans. Willie immediately goes to Maggie to try to explain himself, but Joe threatens to kill him if he ever comes near Maggie again.

EPISODE 272
Barnabas reveals to Willie that he is a vampire no longer. Julia convinces Lang to let her be his assistant instead of Willie. Jeff tells Lang his dream and then Lang is the third person to experience it.

EPISODE 273
Barnabas plans to be transferred into another body and even sends a message to Collinwood, stating that he will be returning to England while another cousin, Adam, will come to live at the Old House. Lang tells Julia is dream and then they begin the experiment.

EPISODE 274
Cassandra uses a voodoo doll to disrupt the experiment. In extreme pain, Lang halts the experiment. Dying, he leaves a message on a tape recorder that Julia must continue the experiment for him. That night, Julia has the horrible dream.

EPISODE 275
Julia is afraid to tell Mrs. Johnson about her dream. Meanwhile, Barnabas insists that Julia continue the experiment. Professor Stokes reveals that a sudden death is the only thing that can end the dream curse.

EPISODE 276
Julia prepares to continue the experiment, but she first feels that she must tell Mrs. Johnson about her dream. Barnabas forbids it.

EPISODE 277
David returns from Boston and meets his new stepmother, Cassandra. Tony suspects that he is somehow being controlled by the woman. When David sees Cassandra secretly meet Tony, he threatens to tell his father.

EPISODE 278
Cassandra strikes David mute so he cannot tell his father what he saw. Julia has the dream again and so Barnabas lets her tell it to Mrs. Johnson.

EPISODE 279
Julia completes the experiment, but it fails. However, Adam does come to life and exhibits violent tendencies.

EPISODE 280
Adam calms down and Julia tells Barnabas that by giving him life, Adam is now their responsibility. Cassandra removes her spell from David, who is now wiser for the experience. Mrs. Johnson has the next dream in the cycle of the curse.

EPISODE 281
Adam is taken to the Old House, but Willie doesn't like him. Willie burns Adam with a cigarette and the patchwork man escapes, although he is found and returned by Barnabas.

EPISODE 282
Julia threatens to return Willie to the Windcliff asylum. Willie shows Adam Josette's earrings. Then Willie manages to slip them into Maggie' purse.

EPISODE 283
Adam speaks his first word, which is "Barnabas." Later, Adam escapes and meets David in the woods. Roger and Barnabas search for David. Adam is shot in the arm by Roger, while David runs into the arms of Barnabas.

EPISODE 284
Julia treats Adam's arm wound. Roger suspects that Barnabas knows who Adam is. Adam befriends Julia.

EPISODE 285
Mrs. Johnson returns from Boston and tells David the dream. Maggie visits Willie and is wearing Josette's earrings. David has the next dream.

EPISODE 286
David tells Willie his dream and now Willie is terrified that he'll have it. Barnabas plots to destroy Cassandra. He tells Willie to steal the portrait of Angelique and then hires Sam Evans to make the portrait look 200 years older. Cassandra begins to age quickly.

EPISODE 287
Cassandra asks Tony to help her find the artist who is aging the portrait. When she learns that it is Sam, she tries to stop him. Sam throws her out, but she returns and strikes him blind.

EPISODE 288
Maggie has Julia examine her father, Sam. Julia pronounces the blindness to be permanent. Barnabas blames Willie for stealing Josette's earrings. Adam chases Willie, but Barnabas beats Adam with his cane.

Jonathan Frid and Grayson Hall

Kathryn Leigh Scott

EPISODE 289
Adam strangles Barnabas and escape, but Julia revives him. They go in search of him, but Adam has gone to Collinwood and kidnapped Carolyn.

EPISODE 290
Tony helps Elizabeth search for Carolyn. Liz suspects that Willie might know who Adam is. Adam takes Carolyn to an underground shed. Willie has the next dream.

EPISODE 291
Julia tries to calm Willie by hypnotizing him, but Willie can't forget the dream. The sheriff begins to suspect that Julia and Willie know who Adam is. Adam is captured by the police.

EPISODE 292
Victoria Winters and Elizabeth attempt to interrogate Adam about where Carolyn is. Cassandra confronts Vicki and asks her why she doesn't like her. Carolyn can't escape, but Adam does, by bending the bars of his prison.

EPISODE 293
The sheriff questions Barnabas about the missing Adam. Adam returns to where he has Carolyn trapped, then carries her to Widow's Hill. Barnabas and the police catch up with them. Adam releases Carolyn and them leaps from Widow's Hill.

EPISODE 294
Barnabas refuses to believe that Adam is really dead. Willie is still upset by his dream and breaks into Carolyn's room to tell her about it. Elizabeth prevents Willie from finishing.

EPISODE 295
Carolyn has part of the dream. Professor Stokes hypnotizes Carolyn in order to place himself in her dream in order to try and end the curse.

EPISODE 296
Stokes has the next dream, but fights it. Angelique appears and tries to control him, but Stokes refuses to be controlled. The dream ends.

EPISODE 297
Cassandra wants Stokes to die and tries to have Tony poison him. But Stokes is suspicious and Tony drinks the poisoned glass instead. Julia revives tony. Stokes, Julia and Tony hold a seance to contact Reverend Trask.

EPISODE 298
In the Old House, the bricks in the wall where Trask was entombed in the past, begin to move. His skeleton is revealed and later he appears in human form. He gets his revenge on Barnabas and ties the now human Barnabas up in Trask's old tomb.

EPISODE 299
Trask puts Barnabas on trial. The ghosts of Nathan Forbes, Suki Forbes, Ruby Tate and Maude Browning are summoned to testify. Adam is still alive and is with Sam Evans. Adam senses that Barnabas is in trouble. Julia discovers that the wall has been bricked up.

EPISODE 300
Cassandra tries to induce Sam Evans into having the dream, but Stokes prevents this. Elizabeth catches Cassandra kissing Tony and threatens to tell Roger. Cassandra puts Elizabeth under a spell which makes her think of nothing except her own death.

EPISODE 301
Barnabas, chained in the wall by the ghost of Trask, taps on it to try to get Willie's attention, but is ignored. Maggie visits Willie at the Old House, but when Joe learns of it, he beats Willie up.

EPISODE 302
Maggie tends to Willie's injuries. Adam, who has been staying with Sam, tries to attack Maggie. Sam tries to calm Adam, but then Adam turns on him, knocking him unconscious. The ghost of Josette sobs in front of the brick tomb of the basement in the Old House. Julia suddenly realizes that Barnabas is behind the wall.

EPISODE 303
Willie breaks down the wall and Julia revives the stricken Barnabas. Julia convinces the ghost of Trask to take his revenge on Cassandra/Angelique. Now Liz thinks she is her ancestor, Naomi, so Cassandra brings Liz to the mausoleum and shows her the grave of Naomi Collins.

EPISODE 304
Trask tries to burn Cassandra in the mausoleum, but her power is stronger than his. Cassandra appears in the hospital where Sam Evans is and induces him to have the dream, thus continuing the cycle.

EPISODE 305
Sam summons Vicki to the hospital, but dies before he can relate the entire dream to her, resulting in the end of the dream cycle. Stokes sees Adam and waits for him at the cottage.

EPISODE 306
Liz is still obsessed with death. Trask captures Cassandra, ties her to a tree and perform an exorcism. Cassandra fades away.

EPISODE 307
Cassandra may be gone, but her curse remains with Liz. While Julia is convinced that Cassandra is really gone, Barnabas isn't so sure. Liz re-enacts the night that Naomi took poison. Barnabas attempts to convince Liz that she is not Naomi, but she collapses in his arms.

EPISODE 308
Julia saves Liz from the effects of the poison, but Julia explains to Roger that while Liz will live, she is still mentally unbalanced. Liz is sent to Windcliff. Roger is concerned that his wife has not returned, while Nicholas Blair arrives and announces that he is Cassandra's brother.

EPISODE 309
Nicholas states that Cassandra will return. He goes to the Old House where he hypnotizes Willie, who reveals that Trask is bricked up in the cellar wall. Nicholas summons Trask from the tomb.

EPISODE 310
Trask refuses to reveal important details of the exorcism. Jeff tells Vicki that his trip was a failure and still has amnesia. Trask appears to them and Jeff recognizes him. Now Vicki is convinced that Jeff is Peter Bradford.

EPISODE 311
Jeff doesn't remember seeing Trask. Maggie and Joe find the cottage in a shambles. Jeff dreams about Nathan Forbes. Joe wakes him up and Jeff attacks him.

EPISODE 312
Jeff comes to his senses and sees that Joe is not Nathan Forbes. Nicholas uses Vicki to lead him to where Trask exorcised Cassandra.

EPISODE 313
Nicholas returns Cassandra to physical existence. Jeff finds Vicki wandering in the woods, holding a button from the jacket worn by Nicholas.

EPISODE 314
Nicholas reveals that the portrait of Angelique has been restored. Jeff questions Nicholas about the button. Adam reveals to Stokes that he was once chained up at the Old House. Stokes tells Vicki to leave town or else she'll have the dream.

EPISODE 315
Jeff tells Vicki to stay with Maggie instead of leaving town. Angelique appears at the cottage and Maggie sees her over Vicki's bed.

EPISODE 316
Vicki discovers that rosewater was left by Angelique and would have induced the dream had she drunk it. Stokes questions Adam about his hatred for Barnabas and Willie. Joe comes to Stokes' house with a gun. Adam flees, with Joe in pursuit.

EPISODE 317
Vicki tells Barnabas that Cassandra has returned. Joe confronts Adam with the rifle, but Adam overpowers him and hits him on the head. Cassandra brings back the ghost of Sam Evans and his spirit tells Vicki the dream.

EPISODE 318
Joe's severely injured body falls out of a closet at the Old House. Willie and Barnabas take him to the hospital. Vicki has the dream and Barnabas is her beckoner.

EPISODE 319
Maggie learns about Joe's accident. Joe tells the sheriff what happened. Nicholas meets Maggie and finds her very attractive.

EPISODE 320
Cassandra leaves a note for Barnabas which appears to have been written by Vicki. Barnabas goes to Vicki, but Julia keeps them apart. Adam returns to the place he held Carolyn captive. Carolyn also returns there and befriends Adam.

EPISODE 321
Barnabas forces Vicki to tell him the dream. Julia slaps Cassandra across the face for causing the dream. Barnabas has the dream, but awakens unharmed. He thinks he has escaped the curse, but when he goes to the door and bat comes in and bites him on the neck.

EPISODE 322
Julia examines Barnabas and thinks he's dead. Adam also seems to be dying. Julia cannot bring herself to drive a stake through Barnabas' heart. Willie and Julia bury him.

EPISODE 323
Willie tells Maggie that Barnabas has died. Julia goes to Adam and realizes that if Adam is still alive, then Barnabas must be also, as their lifeforces were linked by the experiment that gave Adam life.

EPISODE 324
Barnabas is still alive within his coffin. Stokes and Julia dig up his grave and find that he is still human. He goes to Cassandra to prove that her dream curse has failed.

EPISODE 325
Carolyn hides Adam in Collinwood. David discovers the tape recording left by Lang telling Julia to carry on his experiment. Nicholas gives Cassandra until midnight to prove herself.

EPISODE 326
Nicholas gives Cassandra a warning by changing her hand to skeleton form. Cassandra tries to force Willie to tell her how Barnabas escaped her dream curse. David plays Dr. Lang's recording for Cassandra.

EPISODE 327
Cassandra plays the tape for Nicholas and he decides not to destroy her. He also restores her hand to normal. David tells Julia bout the taped message, but when he plays it for her, the tape is different.

EPISODE 328
Julia tells Barnabas about the tape. Mrs. Johnson argues with Harry about food missing from the kitchen. Carolyn sneaks Adam his breakfast and he reads lines from a love poem. Barnabas questions Carolyn about Adam's whereabouts. Harry overhears them and breaks into the west wing.

EPISODE 329
Harry pulls a knife on Adam, who overpowers him, trying to end his life, but Carolyn stops him. Adam tries to kill Carolyn. Nicholas summons the ghost of Dr. Lang and learns that Julia brought Adam to life.

EPISODE 330
Nicholas meets Stokes and questions him about Adam. Julia tries to get Stokes to tell her where Adam is, but she ends up answering questions about Barnabas' dream. Nicholas summons the dead bodies that were used to create Adam and commands them to lead him to Adam. The bodies point to Collinwood.

EPISODE 331
Nicholas finds Adam and befriends him. Nicholas promises Carolyn that he'll keep Adam's whereabouts a secret. Cassandra finds Adam and tries to kill him with an axe.

EPISODE 332
Nicholas stops Cassandra from killing Adam. When Cassandra attempts to use voodoo on Adam, Nicholas takes away her powers. She goes to Barnabas and tries to shoot him.

EPISODE 333
Cassandra confesses to Barnabas that she is really Angelique. Suddenly she begins to age, as does her portrait. Cassandra runs back to Collinwood, but Roger doesn't even recognize her. Julia and Barnabas come to Collinwood, but Cassandra seems to have left.

EPISODE 334
Cassandra goes to Vicki's room to get her portrait. Nicholas agrees to save her only if she can get Barnabas to forgive her. Barnabas refuses and she dies.

EPISODE 335
Carolyn convinces Adam that he only dreamed that Cassandra tried to kill him. Roger shows Nicholas a house that he can move into. Adam tries to force himself on Carolyn. Nicholas brings the coffin of Angelique to the basement of his home.

EPISODE 336
Jeff gives Vicki an engagement ring. Stokes tries to make Adam understand that Carolyn doesn't love him, also revealing what Adam really is. In a rage, Adam tries to stab him.

EPISODE 337
Harry stops Adam from committing suicide. Adam goes to Barnabas and demands that a mate be created for him.

EPISODE 338
Barnabas explains that Lang created him and Julia only finished his experiment. Adam still demands a mate. Vicki reveals to Barnabas that she is marrying Jeff. Vicki is returning to Collinwood when Adam attacks her.

EPISODE 339
Adam brings Vicki to the west wing. He states that she'll remain there until Barnabas gives him what he wants.

EPISODE 340
Barnabas and Jeff search the woods for Vicki. Tom Jennings is working in the basement of Nicholas Blair's home and finds the coffin of Angelique. Nicholas says that it is empty and was there when he moved in. Later, Tom is attacked in the woods. Jeff discovers the body and finds fang marks on the neck.

EPISODE 341
Adam shows Nicholas where he is holding Vicki captive. Nicholas tells Jeff that he saw Barnabas running from the woods. Adam drugs Vicki to make her sleep.

EPISODE 342
Vicki is taken to the home of Nicholas Blair. He releases Angelique from her coffin. Angelique is now a vampire. Nicholas insists that she obey him and not attack Barnabas. Angelique appears to Vicki and takes the engagement ring. Adam takes the ring to Barnabas and states that unless he creates a mate for him, Vicki will die.

EPISODE 343
Barnabas tries to convince Julia to create the mate for Adam, but she refuses. Stokes tries to get Adam to reveal where Vicki is. Adam states that he must have a mate that will love him, or Vicki will die.

EPISODE 344
Julia tells Barnabas that Tom is close to death. Adam comes to Nicholas and wants to free Vicki, but Nicholas talks him out of it. Julia agrees to create Eve if Vicki is released. Adam agrees, but threatens to kill the entire Collins family if Barnabas and Julia are lying.

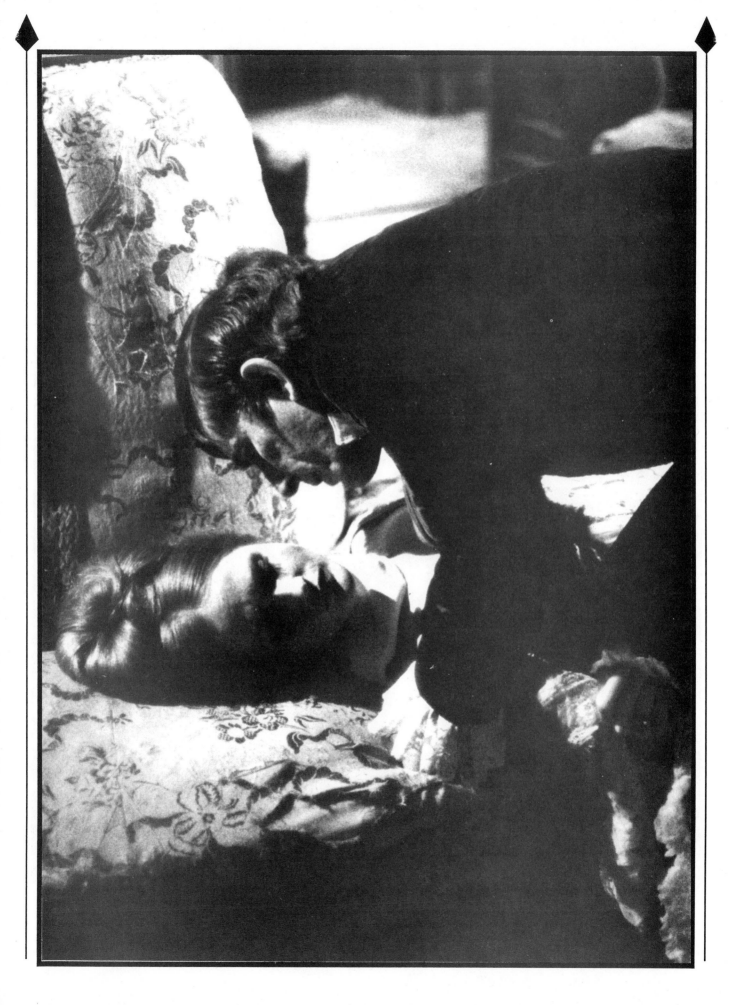

David Henesy as David Collins

EPISODE 345
Nicholas frees Vicki. He visits Maggie, and Joe stops by after being released from the hospital. Nicholas order Angelique to attack Joe.

EPISODE 346
Julia tells Barnabas that Vicki is back at Collinwood. Barnabas orders Willie to dig up a grave to get a body for the experiment. Joe asks Barnabas about Nicholas Blair. Willie wants to leave Collinwood for good, but Barnabas talks him out of it. Joe visits Angelique at Blair's house. Angelique bites Joe on the neck.

EPISODE 347
Nicholas is happy with what Angelique has done. Julia prepares to create Eve. Angelique summons Joe. On the way, Joe stumbles on Willie digging up a grave.

EPISODE 348
Willie can't explain what he's been caught doing. Joe threatens to go to the police, but Nicholas orders him not to. Nicholas fears that when Tom comes out of his coma he'll tell about Angelique's coffin.

EPISODE 349
Maggie visits Tom in the hospital, and he tells her about the coffin. Angelique summons Joe and sends him to visit Tom. Joe opens the window in Tom's room and Angelique bites him again.

EPISODE 350
Joe tells Julia that tom is Dead. Willie threatens to kill Adam. Barnabas fears that Tom will become a vampire and forces Willie to dig up Tom's grave, but when they open the coffin, they find he's gone.

EPISODE 351
Barnabas tells Julia that Tom has returned from the grave. Vicki visits Barnabas and he returns the ring Adam had taken from her. Jeff finds Lang's journal. Tom breaks into the Old House and attacks Julia.

EPISODE 352
Willie finds Julia unconscious, but when she comes to she forces him not to tell Barnabas what happened. She returns to Collinwood and that night tells Willie she can't continue with the creation of Eve. Julia goes to the woods and Tom bites her again.

EPISODE 353
Barnabas discovers the marks on Julia's neck and vows to destroy Tom. Vicki and Jeff encounter Adam and Jeff is knocked unconscious. Vicki starts to remember who kidnapped her. Julia tries to stall Adam by saying she is ill and needs more time for the experiment. Jeff breaks into the lab and finds the body being prepared for the experiment.

EPISODE 354
Barnabas discovers Jeff in the lab. He convinces Jeff not to go to the police because of the threats Adam has made against everyone. Roger tells Barnabas that Liz escaped from Windcliff. Barnabas sets a trap for Tom, but it fails.

EPISODE 355
Liz is found in the woods by Roger. Julia goes to Tom's tomb and Liz follows. Tom bites Julia again.

EPISODE 356
Liz tells Barnabas that she has seen her coffin. Barnabas finds Julia in the tomb and returns her to the Old House. Later he returns to the tomb to battle Tom.

EPISODE 357
Barnabas drives a stake through Tom's heart. Roger wants to prove to Liz that her story about the coffin is false. Nicholas comes to the tomb and removes the coffin. When Roger and Barnabas come to the tomb, Barnabas is shocked to see that the coffin is missing.

EPISODE 358
Julia recovers and goes to visit Maggie, who is concerned about Joe. After Julia leaves, Joe shows up and begs Maggie to confine him to the cottage. Angelique summons Joe and he cannot resist. He pushes Maggie aside and goes to Blair's house.

EPISODE 359
Barnabas is at Blair's house when Joe arrives. He realizes that something is wrong with Joe and forces him to leave with him. Joe returns to Maggie and apologizes. Angelique summons him again and he leaves. Nicholas comes to the cottage and he and Maggie both notice that Joe is gone.

EPISODE 360
Joe has returned to Blair's house. Angelique bites him again. Maggie comes to Joe's apartment and demands an explanation. Willie comes to see Maggie and tells her of his woes, but they are interrupted by Nicholas. At Blair's house, Nicholas contacts Willie through a mirror. Willie explains that the experiment needs a woman for the life force.

EPISODE 361
Nicholas wants Angelique to be the life force for Eve. Adam comes to the Old House to check on the experiments in progress. Jeff reveals to Adam that he was the one who dug up graves to give him life. Angelique comes to the Old House to tell Jeff that she will be the life force of Eve.

EPISODE 362
Angelique bites Jeff again and tries to get him to begin the experiment without Julia. Roger offers Jeff a job, but is turned down. Liz dreams about being buried alive.

EPISODE 363
Liz contacts Tony Peterson to make changes in her will. Adam sees Tony and Carolyn kissing on the terrace. In a jealous rage, he attacks Tony.

EPISODE 364
Carolyn finds Tony knocked unconscious. When Tony awakens, he cannot remember who attacked him. Roger is shocked to learn about the changes Liz has made in her will. Adam escapes from the west wing of Collinwood.

EPISODE 365
Julia finds Jeff reading Lang's notebook. Stokes tells Barnabas that Adam has escaped. Vicki returns her engagement ring to Jeff. Julia prepares for the creation of Eve.

EPISODE 366
Adam comes to Blair's house and wants to halt the experiment, but Nicholas talks him out of it. Nicholas catches Angelique using his mirror to learn about the experiment. Angelique goes to the cellar of the Old House and bites Jeff.

EPISODE 367
Angelique tells Jeff that he must try the experiment using her life force Carolyn presents Adam with a gift and he is overjoyed. Jeff begins the experiment.

EPISODE 368
Barnabas interrupts Jeff in the middle of the experiment. Angelique vanishes, leaving Jeff to explain what he's doing. He tells Barnabas that he was just simulating the experiment. Barnabas asks him to leave, and decides to use Maggie as the life force. When Willie learns of this, he tries to destroy the body.

EPISODE 369
Barnabas stops Willie and reminds him that Adam will key everyone if they fail for any reason. Adam states that he will kill Vicki if they do not get the life force that night. Willie uses chloroform on Maggie and flees with her just as Barnabas arrives at the cottage.

EPISODE 370
Barnabas tells Julia that Maggie has disappeared. Willie takes Maggie to the secret room of the mausoleum. In flashback, Maggie remembers when Julia took her to the same place.

EPISODE 371

Barnabas vows to kill Adam with a rifle. Adam beat up Barnabas and then goes to Collinwood and strangles Vicki.

EPISODE 372

Barnabas and Carolyn save Vicki. Carolyn wants to know how Barnabas knew that Vicki was in danger, but he refuses to say. Adam tells Nicholas that Maggie is supposed to be the life force, but Nicholas wants Carolyn to be the life force instead.

EPISODE 373

Adam comes to the Old House demanding that Carolyn be used as the life force. Maggie tries to escape from the secret room, but Willie stops her. Nicholas hypnotizes Willie and tells him to free Maggie. In flashback, Maggie remembers dining with Barnabas.

EPISODE 374

Maggie begins to remember everything Barnabas ever did to her, just as Willie comes to free her. Nicholas hypnotizes Carolyn and tells her to be the life force for Eve. Maggie grills Willie about the past, and in flashback she remembers being put in a coffin by Barnabas.

EPISODE 375

Maggie reveals that she knows what Barnabas is. Willie tries to convince her that it was a dream. Vicki thinks that Adam was the man who strangled her. Carolyn abruptly shows up at the Old House and announces that she will be the life force for Eve. Willie tells Barnabas that Maggie remembers everything.

EPISODE 376

Barnabas tells Julia that Maggie must be hypnotized again. Adam prevents Julia from leaving. Willie tries to shoot Adam, but Adam takes the gun away from him. Julia prepares the experiment.

EPISODE 377

Adam tries to get Carolyn to marry him instead of doing the experiment, but she refuses. Carolyn comes to the lab and the experiment begins. Something malfunctions and Julia says that Carolyn may die.

EPISODE 378

Adam carries Carolyn to Josette's room. Carolyn describes what it felt like when her life force was being drained, then she collapses. Adam is enraged and attacks Barnabas. Adam leaves and Julia goes to Josette's room, but discovers that Carolyn is gone.

EPISODE 379

Barnabas thinks that Adam took Carolyn's body. Maggie wakes up and opens the secret room just as Julia enters. Julia tries to hypnotize Maggie, but she recognizes the medallion and realizes that Julia erased her memory before. Barnabas goes to Collinwood to announce that Carolyn is dead.

EPISODE 380

Carolyn greets Barnabas at Collinwood. She'd only fainted before. Nicholas tells Adam that he will provide another life force for Eve. With Carolyn's help, Nicholas contacts the spirit of Leona Eltridge. When she appears, Nicholas tells her to return to human form at 3 AM,

EPISODE 381

Adam brings Leona Eltridge to the Old House. He tells Barnabas that she will be the life force for Eve. Julia performs the experiment again. This time Leona dies and Eve comes to life.

EPISODE 382

Adam is at first not pleased with Even because she does not look like Carolyn. Eve begins to speak as Stokes arrives to inform them that the name Leona Eltridge is really an anagram of Danielle Roget, one of the most evil women of the 18th Century, and that her spirit is now living in Eve.

EPISODE 383: Stokes and Barnabas question Eve but learn nothing. They are visited by spirits who lead them to the basement room where they discover Leonas' dead body is gone. Adam and Eve are also gone.

EPISODE 384: Stokes goes to the west wing to find Adam, but finds David there instead. Later, David goes to the cemetery as Willie ties Maggie up in the secret room. David frees Maggie, Willie returns and is shocked at what David did.

EPISODE 385: Willie reports to Barnabas that Maggie has escaped from the secret room. Angelique bites Joe just as Maggie enters Joe's apartment. Maggie tries to convince Joe to leave town. Joe goes to Barnabas and tells him that Maggie wants to see him. Barnabas believes that Maggie will tell the police everything. However, when Willie and Barnabas arrive at the cottage, Maggie simply gives them some sketches that her father did of Barnabas.

EPISODE 386: Barnabas suspects that Nicholas erased Maggie's memory. Eve informs Nicholas that she cannot stand the sight of Adam and wants to kill him. Stokes, Barnabas and Julia are visited by spirits again. During a seance, the spirit of Phillipe Cordier speaks through Barnabas. The spirit informs them that he is Danielle Roget's lover. The spirit comes to Blair's house and strangles Adam. Barnabas feels like he is being strangled also.

EPISODE 387: Nicholas drives the spirit out of the house and both Adam and Barnabas recover. Harry spies on Barnabas and learns that he plans to kill Eve. Harry reports to Nicholas what he has just learned. Nicholas sends for Angelique.

EPISODE 388: Nicholas is furious to learn that Angelique has gone to Jeff without his permission. He goes to Jeff's apartment and stops Angelique from biting him. Nicholas hypnotizes Jeff into forgetting about Angelique. Adam brings Eve to Blair's House, where she will be safe from Barnabas.

EPISODE 389: Liz reveals her plans for a special mausoleum. Roger comes in and smashes it. Liz hears voices telling her she will die soon. Jeff comes back to Vicki and tries to patch up their engagement. Roger discovers that Liz is missing. Jeff finds her in the graveyard and brings her to the drawing room. Vicki believes that Liz is dead.

EPISODE 390: Julia prepares a special injection to kill Eve. Later, Julia declares that Liz is dead, but Liz suddenly opens her eyes. Vicki decides to give Jeff another chance at their engagement. Julia has a dream that something terrible will happen to Barnabas when he attempts to kill Eve.

EPISODE 391: Julia tells Barnabas about her dream, and warns him not to go to Blair's house. Stokes comes to Blair's house to invite him to Barnabas' dinner party and he accepts. During the party, Julia comes in with the excuse that Liz is ill and asks for Barnabas. Barnabas excuses himself and leaves for Blair's house. He goes into Eve's room, where Angelique is waiting for him.

EPISODE 392: Angelique attacks Barnabas and he is now under her power. Nicholas orders Angelique not to see Barnabas again without his permission. Barnabas returns to the old house and reports to Stokes and Julia that their plan did not work. Angelique disobeys orders and bites Barnabas again,.

EPISODE 393: Nicholas discovers that Adam is suffering from the same neck wounds as Barnabas. Joe comes to Angelique, but she no longer wants him. In a rage, Joe stabs himself with a letter opener.

EPISODE 394: Angelique summons Barnabas to take Joe's body to the woods to die. Barnabas brings him to Julia instead. She discovers the wounds on his neck. Julia suspects that Cassandra has returned as a vampire.

EPISODE 395: Adam and Even come to visit Carolyn at the west wing of Collinwood. Jeff is waiting for Vicki at the same time. David is angry at Jeff for wanting to take Vicki away. Eve appears before Jeff and calls him Peter Bradford.

EPISODE 396: Eve tells Jeff that they both lived before. Vicki informs Liz that she will marry Jeff. Nicholas sends Eve back to 1795, where she is reunited with Peter.

EPISODE 397: Nicholas tells Eve about Phillipe. Eve comes to Jeff and tells him that he will never marry Vicki. Nicholas comes to Maggies' to propose. Maggie refuses.

EPISODE 398: Harry is sent to the old house by Nicholas to put poison in Joe's medicine. Angelique summons Barnabas and orders him to force Joe to take the poisoned medicine. Angelique then bites Barnabas again.

Grayson Hall

EPISODE 399: Julie comes in and catches Barnabas attempting to give Joe the medicine. Joe overhears Julie telling Barnabas that the medicine is poison. Later that evening, Joe tries to strangle Barnabas.

EPISODE 400: Mrs. Johnson stops Joe from killing Barnabas. Roger talks Liz into inspecting the mausoleum at Eagle Hill to see if it can be changed to suit her purpose. When they enter, they find Joe Haskell unconscious. They bring him into the drawing room, where he confesses to having attempted to kill Barnabas.

EPISODE 401: Sheriff Patterson questions Mrs Johnson, Julia, and Barnabas about Joe. Angelique comes to Barnabas and bites him again.

EPISODE 402: Julie discovers the wounds on Barnabas' neck. Willie and Julia take Barnabas to the basement cell. Later, Barnabas remembers the secret passageway that Maggie once found. He hits Willie over the head and escapes through it.

EPISODE 403: Vicki and Jeff decided to get married by the end of the month. Even comes to Jeff and tries to convince him he is Peter Bradford. Roger sees them kissing. Jeff convinces Roger not to tell Vicki. Later that evening, Roger has a dream about the wedding and is determined to stop it.

EPISODE 404: Roger describes his dream to Vicki. Barnabas is brought to a hut near the sea where Angelique plans to go away with him. Julia informs Roger that Barnabas is missing. Barnabas tried to go to Vicki. Some technical problems here.

EPISODE 405: Vicki finds Barnabas in the woods and brings him to the west wing. Julia visits Joe in the hospital and tries to get him to tell her who attacked him. After Joe refuses to tell her, she goes to Blair's house. Nicholas won't give her any information. When Julia leave's Blair's house, she sees Angelique in the woods.

EPISODE 406: Julia goes back into Blair's house and finds Adam suffering like Barnabas. Vicki brings a crucifix to Barnabas. Angelique summons Barnabas through the mirror, but sees the cross and can do nothing. She sends Adam to the west wing and he gets the cross away from Barnabas. Then Barnabas goes to Angelique.

EPISODE 407: Willie and Julia go out and search for Barnabas. Nicholas discovers that Angelique has stolen his mirror. Nicholas decides to destroy Angelique. Willie finds Barnabas in the woods and brings him to the old house. Nicholas goes to drive a stake through Angelique's heart, but the coffin is empty.

EPISODE 408: Angelique outsmarted Nicholas by moving to a different coffin. Through the mirror, Angelique learns that Barnabas has been sent to a hospital (Windcliff) far away. Eve is sent to watch Jeff and she runs into Angelique, who bargains with her. Angelique agrees to send Eve back to the year 1795 if she agrees to protect her during the day. Angelique begins the ceremony. Eve vanishes.

EPISODE 409: The year is 1795. Eve appears in the Collinsport Jail. She demands to see Peter. She tells him that she will help him escape. Joshua orders Ben to destroy the family history book that Vicki brought with her. Eve meets Ben in the woods and tells him about her escape plan. Ben gives her the book to hold for him. Peter does not want to escape and writes Eve a note. She reads the note as Peter goes to the gallows. Eve vanishes.

EPISODE 410: Nicholas wonders where Eve is. When he turns his back, Eve appears. She explains that she was taking a walk. Nicholas questions her about the history book she is holding and warns her that she must do better at making Adam happy. Vicki prepares for her wedding day as Eve prepares to stop it. Vicki opens a present sent by Eve. Elizabeth looks at the card, and it says, "Peter".

EPISODE 411: Eve comes to Jeff at the terrace and she gives him the note from Peter. Jeff tells Roger that he must see Vicki. Jeff tells Vicki that he cannot marry her. He shows her the note. Jeff races off to the cemetery and finds the grave of Peter Bradford.

EPISODE 412: Jeff digs up Peter's grave and finds it empty. Vicki has a dream about the past. Adam kills Eve. Jeff finds Eve's body in the closet.

EPISODE 413: Vicki tries to convince Peter to wait for the police. Angelique tries to enlist Adam's aid. Joe and Julia meet Chris and think he is Tom. Julia learns of Eve's death. Angelique tries to get Nicholas in trouble with his master.

EPISODE 414: Angelique visits Hell and tells Diabolos that Nicholas is in love with Maggie. Julia tells Nicholas that Eve is dead. Maggie visits Nicholas and then becomes possessed by Diabolos.

EPISODE 415: Diabolos confronts Nicholas about Maggie and Eve. Nicholas is ordered to sacrifice Maggie in a Black Mass.

EPISODE 416: Nicholas tells Barnabas about the new experiment to bring Eve back to life. Nicholas read's Maggie's fortune and then proposes to her. Vicki learns of this and confronts Nicholas. Nicholas puls the stake out of Tom's heart and sends him to attack Vicki.

EPISODE 417: Barnabas saves Vicki from Tom. Chris comes to Blair's house to warn Nicholas not to harm Vicki or marry Maggie if he wants the experiment to succeed. Nicholas forces harry to dig up Eve's grave. Barnabas confronts Tom with a crucifix. As the sun rises, Tom vanishes forever.

EPISODE 418: Maggie accepts Nicholas' proposal Chris visits his little sister, Amy, at Windcliff. Amy is happy to hear that Chris is going to stay in Collinsport. Chris asks the innkeeper to lock him in his room. The innkeeper hears strange noises coming from Chris' room and enters it. Nicholas begins the ceremony to make Maggie his bride.

EPISODE 419: Nicholas brings Maggie to the old house to provide the life force for the new Eve. The experiment begins. Barnabas breaks all the equipment. Nicholas tries to stop him, but he has lost his powers. Adam is horrified to see that Eve has turned into skeleton form. Barnabas witnesses the destruction of Nicholas.

EPISODE 420: Adam goes to Collinwood to kidnap Vicki. He brings her to the lab and tries to do the experiment himself. In an effort to save Vicki, Barnabas shoots Adam, even though he may revert back to what he was before.

EPISODE 421: Adam is wounded, but not killed. He goes to Stokes, who prepares him to be sent to a clinic to have his scars removed. Jeff comes to Stokes with a special potion that helps him discover that he is Peter Bradford.

EPISODE 422: Vicki and Jeff are married. Barnabas and Julia decide to drive a state through Angelique's heart. When they go to her coffin, it is empty. Vicki watches in horror, as Jeff fades away, back to his own time.

EPISODE 423: Vicki returns to Collinwood. She informs Liz that Jeff has gone back to his own time. Chris argues with Julia about Amy. Julia tells Maggie that Nicholas has gone away. Liz is on her way to the old house when she hears an animal growling.

EPISODE 424: Amy appears in the woods and the animal goes away. Liz is grateful to Amy and brings her to Collinwood. David meets Amy and they explore the west wing. Amy talks to Quentin Collins on an old telephone that is not even connected.

EPISODE 425: Amy goes to the west wing to meet Quentin, but he does not appear. David and Amy hold an unsuccessful seance to contact Quentin. Chris comes to Collinwood to visit Amy. Carolyn and Chris go out for a drink at the Blue Whale. Later that evening, the barmaid is attacked by a werewolf.

EPISODE 426: Any is awakened by a dream about Chris. Vicki notices that Jeff is trying to contact her. Stokes tries to convince her to forget about Jeff. He tells her that the only way she can be with him is to die. Amy is awakened by the widow's crying. Vicki goes to Widows' Hill and prepares to jump.
EPISODE 427: Vicki is convinced not to jump by Liz and Stokes. Stokes is determined to hold a seance to contact Jeff. Stokes meets Chris and convinces him to stay for the seance. During the seance, the spirit of Magda speaks through Carolyn. She warns them of a spirit that must not come back. Chris grabs Carolyn and stops the seance.

EPISODE 428: Carolyn still feels Magda's presence. Amy tells David that Quentin is angry. They contact him through the old telephone and he asks them to find him tonight. Roger finds a letter from Quentin after a book falls from the piano. Spirits visit David and Amy as they enter the west wing.

EPISODE 429: David and Amy are locked in the west wing. Carolyn is awakened by a dream about David and Amy in danger. Roger discovers that David and Amy are missing. Liz, Roger and Carolyn search the west wing. After hearing Quentin's music, David breaks down a panel in a wall to find Quentin.

EPISODE 430: David and Amy find Quentin's skeleton. Liz comes to the old house and asks Barnabas to search the old house for David and Amy. When they do not find them, Liz and Barnabas leave. David and Amy enter the old house and take a baby's cradle. From there, they bring it to the west wing. David and Amy explain to Liz and Barnabas that they were on an adventure. They return to the west wing.

EPISODE 431: David and Amy meet Quentin and Beth Chavez. They do not speak. Quentin possesses David and Beth possesses Amy. David and Any bury Quentin's skeleton. Roger returns and David and Amy plan to kill him.

EPISODE 432: Roger trips down the stairs because of a wire David has tied across it. Liz finds Roger. He is okay and tells Liz about the wire. When he tries to show it to her, it is not there. Liz calls Stokes after finding a Tarot card. Stokes brings Janet Findley to Collinwood. She vows to find the spirit that is possessing the house.

EPISODE 433: David and Amy try to warn Quentin about Mrs. Findley. Joe comes to see Amy. She see the sign of the pentagram on his face. Mrs. Findley finds the secret passage to the west wing. David and Amy lock her in the west wing.

EPISODE 434: The music begins to play for Mrs. Findley but Quentin does not appear. The old telephone rings and she hears breathing, but then discovers that the line is disconnected. A voice informs her that she is going to die. Joe visits Chris to inform him that he is leaving town. Joe tells him about the pentagram Amy saw on his face. Back at Collinwood, Liz and Julia look in horror as Mrs. Findley falls to her death down the great stairs.

EPISODE 435: Vicki is visited by Jeff's spirit. Barnabas proposes to Vicki, but she refuses. Jeff returns in human form. Vicki and Jeff fade away, much to the amazement of Barnabas and Elizabeth.

EPISODE 436: Liz thinks she is going to die. Chris comes to Julia for sleeping pills. Joe pays Chris a visit. When he leaves, Chris transforms into a werewolf.

EPISODE 437: Maggie is hired as the new governess. Amy sees the pentagram again on Joe's face. Joe goes into town to get Maggie's things. At the cottage, Joe is attacked by the werewolf.

EPISODE 438: Barnabas finds Joe in the cottage. He brings him to Collinwood. Chris wonders if Joe is alive. Joe comes to Chris and he see the transformation take place. Joe agreed to shoot Chris after he changed. The shots do not work.

EPISODE 439: A crazed Joe sneaks into Collinwood. Liz has a nightmare and Cassandra tells her that she is going to be buried alive. Amy escapes and runs to Julia. Liz falls into a death-like coma.

EPISODE 440: Any tries to comfort Jeff about his aunt's death. Barnabas informs Mrs. Johnson that no one outside the family is to know that Liz is dead. However, Mr. Jarrett from the funeral home arrives. He informs Barnabas that he received a call from someone that Liz is dead. Quentin made David call, but David denies doing so. Barnabas decides that David and Amy should go on a trip to Boston with him and Maggie.

EPISODE 441: David and Amy play pranks to keep them from having to leave for Boston. Mrs. Johnson believes that they are messages from Vicki. She believes that Vicki wants to return from the past. A real message from Vicki convinces Barnabas to stay at Collinwood and not send the children to Boston.

EPISODE 442: Joe is in jail. Julia and the sheriff are convinced that he is insane. Joe tries to warn them about the danger. Joe has a dream about the night he shot Chris. He sees Tom in the mausoleum and then he is tormented by visions of Tom as a vampire and Chris as a werewolf. Joe wakes up in a straitjacket. Chris waits with Joe until the men in the white coats come and take him to Windcliff.

EPISODE 443: Barnabas shows Julia the message from Vicki. Carolyn is convinced that her mother is still alive. David takes a photo of Barnabas and Carolyn. Vicki's image, hanging, appears in the photo. Harry catches Amy talking on the old telephone. He does not believe Amy when she tells him the truth about Quentin. David shows the photo to Barnabas and Carolyn.

EPISODE 444: Barnabas announces that he will stay at Collinwood to help Vicki. He plans to go back in time to prevent Vicki from being hanged. David and Amy find a new grave next to Peter Bradford's. Later, Barnabas and Julia find a gravestone that is marked, "Victoria Winters."

EPISODE 445: Through a series of flashbacks to the year of 1796, Barnabas explains how he killed Nathan Forbes. He then summons Peter Bradford and pleads with him to bring him back to 1796. Julia watches as Barnabas fades away.

EPISODE 446: The year is 1796. Barnabas meets Ben and informs him that he is going to change history. Barnabas meets Nathan at the "Eagle" and prepares to re-enact the night that Nathan tried to kill him.

EPISODE 447: Barnabas tricks Nathan by being invisible. Nathan's attempt to kill Barnabas fails. Barnabas takes the weapon away from Forbes and then forces him to sign a confession stating that he lied during Vicki's trial. At the docks, Barnabas attacks Crystal. She falls into the water. Back at Collinwood, the body of Crystal shows up in the study.

EPISODE 448: Angelique appears to Barnabas and confesses that she made the body appear. She agrees to save her only if Barnabas agrees to stay in the 18th century with her. Barnabas agrees. Vicki is hung at the gallows. Barnabas and Peter bring her body back to Collinwood. Angelique vows to never bring her back to life.

EPISODE 449: Angelique will release Vicki from her spell after they both leave together. Barnabas does not want to believe her. He has Ben burn Angelique and scatter her ashes to the wind. Vicki comes back to life. Natalie sees Barnabas and finds his empty coffin. Peter and Vicki go away together. Barnabas attempts to return to the present day by having Ben chain him in his coffin. Natalie sees Ben open the secret room. later, Natalie and Forbes come to the secret room to drive a stake through Barnabas' heart.

EPISODE 450: Ben stops Forbes and kills him and Natalie. In the present day, Julia and Willie go to the cemetery. They wait for Barnabas to return. Back in 1796, Ben tells Barnabas that he could not chain him in his coffin until he tells him what to do about the murders he committed. In the present day, Willie goes into the secret room expecting to find Barnabas in his coffin, but he is not there. In 1796, Barnabas has convinced Ben to chain him in his coffin. After Willie leaves the secret room, Barnabas returns in the chained coffin. Back at the old house, Willie begins to hear Barnabas' heart beating.

EPISODE 451: Willie and Julia return to the secret room. They find the chained coffin. Willie releases Barnabas. Back at Collinwood, Carolyn punishes David for being cruel to Amy. David decides to play "the game" with Carolyn.

EPISODE 452: Carolyn convinces Chris to move into Mathew Morgan's (an old caretaker) cottage. Mrs. Johnson catches David and Amy playing "dress up". David and Amy explain that they were just playing. Later, David decides to play "the game" with Mr. Johnson/

EPISODE 453: Mrs. Johnson tells Maggie that the cottage is cursed, but agrees to fix it up for Chris. David locks Mrs. Johnson in the cottage. Quentin appears to her. Maggie finds Mrs. Johnson and bring her back to Collinwood.

EPISODE 454: Amy sees the pentagram on Carolyn's face. Amy pretends to be sick. Maggie goes to the cottage to get Chris, just as he is about to change into a werewolf.

EPISODE 455: Chris tells Maggie that he will come to see Amy. Maggie leaves and Chris changes into the werewolf. Carolyn visits her mother's mausoleum, as Liz comes out of her coma. Liz cannot move or speak, but knows Carolyn is in danger. While walking through the woods, Carolyn hears her mother's voice warning her to go back to Collinwood. The werewolf follows her her there.

EPISODE 456: Carolyn tells Julia that she found Chris' cottage in a shambles. Carolyn goes back to the mausoleum and is attacked by the werewolf. Liz rings her bell in her coffin. Barnabas rescues Carolyn. They open Liz' coffin, but she is not alive. Later, back at Collinwood, Liz shows up.

EPISODE 457: Barnabas goes werewolf hunting. Beth summons Amy to the woods. Barnabas visits Chris at the cottage and tells him about the attack on Carolyn. Amy comes to the cottage and burns Chris' bloodstained shirt.

Another view of Kathryn

*Four
off-camera
views*

EPISODE 458: Barnabas figures out that Chris is the werewolf. He tells Julia. Carolyn brings her friend, Donna, to Collinwood. Chris gets talked into driving Donna back to Bangor. Chris pretends to be ill and gives Donna the keys to his car. Donna comes to the cottage to return the keys as Chris changes into a werewolf. Later, Donna is found dead in the woods.

EPISODE 459: Donna's dead body is brought to the morgue. The sheriff shows Carolyn the body and she is shocked. The sheriff questions Chris and takes him into custody. Barnabas and Julia search the cottage and find Donna's purse. Barnabas tells the sheriff that Chris was drunk and he is released. Back at the cottage, Barnabas tells Chris that he knows he is the werewolf.

EPISODE 460: Barnabas brings Chris to the secret room in the mausoleum. Chris tells Barnabas about the night he first changed into the werewolf. David meets Quentin in the west wing. Quentin wants David to poison Chris. David refuses.

EPISODE 461: Barnabas returns to the secret room and gets Chris. Julia agrees to help Chris. Quentin's spirit puts poison into Chris' drink. Beth leads Julia and Barnabas to Chris cottage. They find him unconscious, but Beth is gone.

EPISODE 462: Julia discovers that Chris has been poisoned. Beth leads Amy to the cottage in a dream. She warns her that Quentin is trying to kill Chris. Amy decides to tell Mrs. Stoddard about Quentin.

EPISODE 463: Before Amy can tell Liz about Quentin, his spirit appease and scares Amy. Liz punishes David and confines him to his room. At night, he sneaks into the west wing and Maggie follows him.

EPISODE 464: Maggie can't find David, so she waits for him in his room. Maggie punishes David and takes his old telephone. David threatens to get even. Maggie hears the old telephone ringing. The windows blow open and her lights go out. Maggie goes looking for David in the west wing and sees Quentin.

EPISODE 465: Maggie is scared and tells Liz about what she saw. Chris and Carolyn search the west wing but find nothing. David shows Liz and Maggie where he hides in west wing. They find a dummy dressed like Quentin. Liz is convinced that Maggie imagined seeing anything else.

EPISODE 466: Maggie has a dream about Quentin killing her. Maggie tells her dream to Barnabas, and he tells her about the night he saw Beth's spirit. Barnabas calls Prof. Stokes. He proposes to hold a seance to contact Mrs. Findley. During the seance, Mrs. FIndley speaks through Mrs. Johnson.

(The episode that follows the one above has been lost by Worldvision Enterprises).

EPISODE 467: Barnabas and Chris open a child's coffin and find a pentagram. Quentin makes David steal the pentagram from Barnabas. Barnabas calls Mr. Ezra Braithwaite to find out who purchased the pentagram. Later, Mr. Braithwaite calls Collinwood and David answers. Quentin takes the phone away from David and hangs it up.

EPISODE 468: Liz informs David that his father is coming home. David does not want to meet him at the airport. Ezra Braithwaite arrives and tells David to get Barnabas. Quentin appears to Ezra. After Ezra realizes who he is, Ezra has a heart attack. Barnabas and David find his dead body.

EPISODE 469: Barnabas believes that Ezra was murdered by the man that Mrs. Johnson and Maggie saw. David has taken Ezra's record book. Roger returns to find Barnabas accusing David of stealing the book. Julia is visit by spirts while searching through some Collins family record books.

EPISODE 470: Julia tries to show Barnabas a photo of Beth, but it is missing. Chris begins to feel that he is changing, even though there is no full moon. Barnabas rushes him to the secret room. Ned Stuart arrives at Collinwood. Carolyn mistakes him for Jeff Clark. Ned goes to the cottage to meet Chris, but he finds Barnabas and Julia instead.

EPISODE 471: Ned Stuart tells Barnabas about his sister who was once going to marry Chris. David runs away after arguing with Maggie. While Maggie is searching for David, she meets Ned. David goes to the mausoleum and begins to open the secret room.

EPISODE 472: Barnabas stops David from opening the secret room. Barnabas brings David back to Collinwood. Barnabas goes back to the secret room and gets Chris. Quentin appears to David. David tells him that he does not want to play the game with him. Quentin touches David's arm. David feels like he is on fire.

EPISODE 473: Maggie finds David unconscious. David utters the name, "Quentin". David runs away as Ned enters. Ned meets Amy. Chris arrives and accuses Ned of putting the poison in his drink. Ned insists that Chris come and see his sister at the inn. David and Amy tell Maggie that they are going to play "dress up" with her. Maggie begins to search for David and Amy. She begins to hear Quentin's laughter.

EPISODE 474: Maggie searches for David and Amy in the study. David and Amy bring Quentin to the study to meet Maggie. Quentin begins to strangle Maggie, but Mrs. Johnson and Liz save her. Mrs. Johnson locks the children up in David's room. Maggie tells Liz that the children are possessed. Quentin's theme begins to play for Liz and Mrs. Johnson. David exclaims that it is too late to be scared.

EPISODE 475: Liz tells Julia about the music and both are convinced that the children are possessed by two ghosts. Chris tells Julia that Sabrina Stuart knows that he is a werewolf. Chris and Julia visit Ned and Sabrina. They are both stunned at her appearance. Ned explains that she has been in shock for two years.

EPISODE 476: Stokes tells Julia that he is going to exorcise Collinwood. Chris informs Carolyn that he must leave Collinwood. Julia convinces Chris not to leave because the spirits that haunt Collinwood must know something about his curse. Stokes performs his exorcism, but it fails. Quentin sets Stokes' room on fire.

EPISODE 477: Stokes smashes the mirror with Quentin's image in it and the flames go out. The ghost of Quentin appears to Roger. Liz and Stokes find Roger in a state of disbelief. Everyone leaves Collinwood and Quentin's laughter is heard throughout Collinwood.

EPISODE 478: Everyone is staying at the old house. Chris reports to Barnabas that he saw Quentin looking at the old house. David and Amy sneak back into Collinwood to destroy the old telephone. Maggie finds David and Amy and brings them back to the old house. That night, Maggie finds that David is gone.

EPISODE 479: Barnabas and Willie search for David and Amy at Collinwood. Maggie follows Amy to Collinwood and Quentin possessed Maggie. Barnabas finds Maggie dressed in a 19th century gown. Maggie can't remember her name and she faints.

EPISODE 480: Barnabas revives Maggie. Ned calls Chris and tells him that Sabrina can speak. Barnabas brings Chris to the secret room and then visits Ned. Barnabas meets Sabrina. Sabrina sees his wolf's head cane and begins to remember what happened to her two years ago.

EPISODE 481: Through a flashback, Sabrina remembers the night she witnessed Chris transformation. Barnabas and Julia go to release Chris. When they open the secret room, Chris is still a werewolf, even though there is no full moon.

EPISODE 482: Barnabas fights the werewolf off with his cane. He closes the room up. Julia believes that the curse has taken complete control over Chris. Amy tells Julie that Quentin may hurt Chris. Julia now believes that there is some connection between Quentin and Chris. Maggie has a dream about Quentin. After hearing about the dream, Barnabas and Maggie search the west wing.

EPISODE 483: Stokes finds a book about the "I-Ching" in the west wing. Maggie tries to get David out of Collinwood, but he falls into a coma. Julia announces that David may die unless they communicate with Quentin. Stokes explains the I-Ching to Barnabas. Barnabas insists on using them to save David. Barnabas throws the words, concentrates on the door, and it opens. Barnabas goes through the door. Julia and Stokes communicate with Barnabas. He tells them that he sees the chained coffin.

EPISODE 484: The year is 1897. Magda and Sandor are at the old house. Magda wants Sandor to steal the Collins' family jewels. Quentin returns to Collinwood and is greeted by the servant, Beth Chavez. Quentin visits his grandmother, Edith, in hopes of learning the family secret and getting the inheritance. Magda believes that the jewels are hidden in the secret room. After seeing a vision of the mausoleum in her crystal ball, Magda sends Sandor to get the jewels. Sandor finds the chained coffin and opens it.

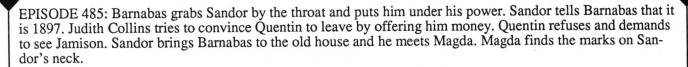

EPISODE 485: Barnabas grabs Sandor by the throat and puts him under his power. Sandor tells Barnabas that it is 1897. Judith Collins tries to convince Quentin to leave by offering him money. Quentin refuses and demands to see Jamison. Sandor brings Barnabas to the old house and he meets Magda. Magda finds the marks on Sandor's neck.

EPISODE 486: Magda realizes that Barnabas is a vampire. Barnabas bargains with Magda by telling her that he can give her jewels. In return, Magda agrees to protect him during the day. Barnabas arrives at Collinwood and introduces himself to Judith. Barnabas meets Quentin. Quentin does not believe Barnabas' story about coming from England. Quentin puts a sword to Barnabas' throat and demands the truth.

EPISODE 487: Judith stops Quentin from harming Barnabas. Judith gives Barnabas her word that she will get Edith to allow him to stay at the old house. At the docks, Barnabas attack Sophie. Back at Collinwood, Quentin sneaks into Edith's room, grabs her by the neck, and demands to know the secret.

EPISODE 488: Judith stops Quentin from harming Edith. Edwards returns with a new governess, Rachel Drummond. Barnabas visits Edith and she exclaims that he is the secret. Edward comes in and tells Barnabas to leave. Edith tries to tell Edward the secret but she just mumbles incoherently.

EPISODE 489: Barnabas meets Carl Collins, who jokes about knowing everything about him. He holds a toy gun to Barnabas' head and demands that he confess. Edith dies and Edward vows to find out what the secret is.

EPISODE 490: Quentin tells Rachel the legends of the tower room. Later, Rachel sees a light in the tower. She tells Edward and he proves to her that she is wrong.

EPISODE 491: While viewing Edith's body, Edward asks Barnabas if he knows the secret. Barnabas denies ever having been told it. Evan Hanley arrives to pay his respects. Quentin convinces Evan to steal Edith's will and then change it to suit his own purposes. Quentin blackmails Evan into doing this by telling him that he is not only a lawyer, but a dealer in black magic as well. Barnabas meets Evan as well as Jamison. Barnabas learns how fond Jamison and Quentin are of each other. Quentin forces Jamison to steal the will that is hidden in Edith's coffin. Barnabas accuses Quentin of stealing the will.

EPISODE 492: Barnabas meets Rachel and tells her that she resembles the portrait of Josette. Quentin begins to hear a strange heartbeat sound. He runs from his room.

EPISODE 493: That night, Quentin dreams of Edith, who tells him to return the stolen will. Quentin awakes, but still hears the heartbeat. Quentin gives the will to Evan. Evan talks Quentin into helping him perform a ritual to summon a spirit to help them deal with Barnabas.

EPISODE 494: During the ceremony, Angelique materializes before them. She soon learns that the year is 1897 and agrees to help Quentin deal with Barnabas. At the old house, Angelique stands before the portrait of Josette and informs Josette that she still hates her. Angelique sees Barnabas with Rachel and is jealous. She fashions a doll out of yarn and begins to strangle it. Rachel begins to choke.

EPISODE 495: Dirk Wilkins enters and interrupts Angelique's spell. Rachel recovers. When Dirk questions, Angelique explains that she is one of Quentin's lady friends. Angelique summons Rachel and brings her to the old house. Barnabas opens his coffin and finds Rachel lying inside it.

EPISODE 496: Barnabas carries Rachel upstairs and questions her. Rachel can't remember how she got to the old house. Rachel hurries back to Collinwood. Barnabas asks Magda for an amulet that will protect Rachel from witchcraft. Rachel sees Beth with a doll. Beth explains that it is for Nora, but later, she brings it to the tower room where Jenny Collins (Quentin's wife) is being hidden.

EPISODE 497: Judith gathers her brothers into the drawing room. She tells them that she has found the will. Edward is shocked to learn that Edith has left everything to Judith. Rachel goes up to the tower room and hears the creaking of a rocker coming from inside.

EPISODE 498: Jenny escapes from the tower room and sets Edward's room on fire. Beth helps him extinguish the flames. Beth and Edward bring Jenny back to the tower room. Later that evening, Rachel goes to the tower room and begins to open the door.

EPISODE 499: Jenny attacks Rachel and renders her unconscious. Jenny escapes and locks Rachel in the tower. Dirk hears Rachel's cries and free her. Judith searches for Jenny and finds herself trapped by the madwoman. Jenny comes at her with a pair of scissors.

EPISODE 500 Judith is saved by Beth. Rachel tells Barnabas that she believes something is hidden in the tower room Barnabas proposes to investigate it himself. Judith locks Jenny in the basement room. Barnabas enters the tower room and begins to search for Rachel's attacker. Suddenly, the doorknob turns and someone begins to open the door.

EPISODE 501: Angelique enters the tower room. She informs Barnabas that she survived the 1796 burning because Satan's power helped her. She downs Barnabas a vision of a dark figure driving a stake through his heart. Then she disappears. Quentin attempts voodoo on Barnabas and sends Jamison to steal his cane. Barnabas begins to feel a pain in his chest. Magda suspects Quentin and breaks in on his ceremony. Magda stops Quentin and tells him that he has the mark of death on him.

EPISODE 502: Magda tells Quentin that he may die tonight. She reads his suture and sees a vision of a woman with a knife. In the basement, Jenny hears the music that Quentin is playing. She realizes Quentin has returned. She vows to punish him for abandoning her. Jenny hits Dirk over the head and escapes. She obtains a large butcher knife and searches for Quentin.

EPISODE 503: Dirk and Beth search for Jenny. At the cottage, Quentin hears a knock at the door. He thinks it is Beth, but it is Jenny. They embrace and Jenny stabs Quentin. Jenny leaves him to die. Later, Dirk finds Quentin's body. Barnabas finds Dirk and thinks he killed Quentin.

EPISODE 504: Barnabas threatens Dirk to tell him about Jenny. Back at Collinwood, Beth takes Jenny back to her basement cell. Jenny tells Beth that she killed Quentin. Barnabas summons Angelique and asks her to save Quentin. Angelique casts a spell over Quentin.

EPISODE 505: Rachel tries to tell Jamison that Quentin is dead, but he runs from his room. Jamison goes to Quentin's room and plays his music. Quentin's spirit possesses Jamison. Jamison tells Carl that he is Quentin. Rachel has a nightmare in which Quentin rises from the dead. She wakes up and finds Quentin sitting in the rocking chair next to her bed.

EPISODE 506: Rachel rushes from her room and shouts that Quentin is there. Carl investigates, but finds nothing. They go to the drawing room and find Quentin's coffin empty. Carl later finds Quentin roaming the upstairs halls. Barnabas tells Judith of a ritual that must be performed to keep Quentin from rising. The ritual is performed and Quentin returns to his coffin. When Carl and Barnabas try to bury him, Quentin rises again. Quentin captures Rachel and caries her off.

EPISODE 507: Barnabas asks Sandor if he knows any way to break a zombie curse. Sandor says that he does not know. Rachel wakes up in Quentin's arms and screams. Magda tells Barnabas that Rachel is missing. Sandor rescues Rachel and brings her to the old house. Quentin comes to the old house and Magda locks him in the basement. Barnabas, Magda and Sandor perform a ceremony to make Quentin's living spirit return to his boy. The ceremony fails and Quentin leaves the old house.

EPISODE 508: Reverend Gregory Trask arrives at the request of Edward to talk with Judith about putting the children in his school. Jamison, still possessed by Quentin, returns and Trask is immediately intrigued with his behavior. Trask tells Judith that the child is possessed and offers his help. Barnabas meets Trask and objects to his offer to help. Judith disagrees. Trask begins to pray for Quentin's spirit to return to its proper place. When Barnabas hears Jamison scream, he bursts into the drawing room.

EPISODE 509: Barnabas finds Trask standing over a kneeling Jamison. Judith insists that Trask continue his work and Barnabas leaves. Trask continues. Later, Barnabas and Judith re-enter the drawing room and they find Quentin and Jamison normal again. Barnabas questions Trask about his great great grandfather, but their conversation is cut short by Judith, who reports that Jamison is missing.

EPISODE 510: Barnabas accuses Quentin of knowing where Jamison is hiding. Quentin does not deny it, because he does not want Jamison to go to Trask's school. Charity Trask arrives (the Rev.'s daughter) and is greeted by Rachel. Barnabas meets Charity and escorts her to her father's room. Rachel tells Barnabas that she attended Trask's school (Worthington Hall) and described the beatings she received after befriending a fellow

Joan Bennett

121

Jonathan Frid

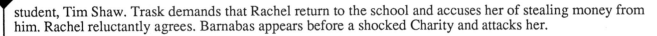

student, Tim Shaw. Trask demands that Rachel return to the school and accuses her of stealing money from him. Rachel reluctantly agrees. Barnabas appears before a shocked Charity and attacks her.

EPISODE 511: Barnabas takes control of Charity. Edward returns and discovers that Edward has run away. Edward finds Quentin going through his papers to try and find out where Jenny is hidden. Edward refuses to tell him. Quentin tries to trade information with him by offering to tell him where Quentin's wife, Laura is. Nora sees a vision of her mother in the fireplace.

EPISODE 512: Edward forbids Nora to mention her mother ever again. Nora goes to her room and sees it in flames. She screams. Edward and Beth run to her room but find no sign of a fire. Nora sneaks out of the house and searches for her mother. When she heads back to the house, a hand is placed on her shoulder.

EPISODE 513: The hand belongs to Nora's and Jamison's mother, Laura Collins. Laura sends Nora inside to get Jamison. Edward refuses to allow Laura to see the children. Edward offers Laura $100,000 to leave and never come back. While Edward is gone to get the money, Quentin comes into the drawing room. When he sees Laura, he shouts that she is dead and she saw her die.

EPISODE 514: Laura laughs at Quentin's claim. She refuses the money that Edward offers. Edward agrees to let her stay. Tim Shaw arrives to take the children to the school. Quentin is in his room, drinking away his troubles. He begs Angelique to appear and help him defeat Laura. Laura comes in on Quentin and he strangles her.

EPISODE 515: A fiery pain shoots through Quentin and he dies. Barnabas informs Angelique that he should not die this way. She agrees to revive Quentin if he announces their engagement.

EPISODE 516: Angelique tells Quentin that he can destroy Laura by finding the urn that contains her power. Mrs. Trask arrives and demands that Rachel return to Worthington Hall. Rachel asks Magda to help her escape.

EPISODE 517: Magda has hidden Rachel in the secret room. At Worthington Hall, Jamison is scolded and locked in a closet by Trask. Magda takes Tim to Rachel. Trask discovers Rachel and Tim.

EPISODE 518: Trask takes Rachel back to the school. Laura comes to the school and tries to get her children. Trask will not give them to her without Edward's permission. Laura vows that her children will not spend one more night in the school. Later that evening, a mysterious fire starts and Nora is trapped in a burning room.

EPISODE 519: Laura appear to Judith in the burning room. Tim rescues both to them. Worthington Hall burns to the ground. Tim takes them to Collinwood. Quentin tells Laura that he knows she caused the fire. Quentin and Magda find Laura's urn. Quentin pours sand into it and Laura collapses.

EPISODE 520: Judith finds Laura very weak. Laura leaves the house when Judith sends for her tea. Laura discovers her urn is missing. Laura prays to Ra and he appears to her in the form of Dirk Wilkins.

EPISODE 521: Jamison returns to Collinwood and becomes angry with Quentin after he learns (from Laura) that Quentin tried to kill his mother. At the old house, Barnabas partakes of Charity's blood. When Barnabas returns Charity to Collinwood, he meets Laura Collins. Barnabas tells Charity that Laura has been dead for over 100 years.

EPISODE 522: Charity is crushed when she meets Angelique and discovers she is engaged to Barnabas. Charity has a dream about her wedding. In the dream, her wedding ceremony turns into a funeral. Judith awakens Charity, but after seeing her reaction to the sunlight, she tells her to stay in bed until her father arrives. Barnabas summons Charity to the old house and they discover a portrait of Jeremiah's first wife, who looks exactly like Laura. Back at Collinwood, Judith and Trask discover the wounds on Charity's neck.

EPISODE 523: Magda tells Barnabas that Trask and Judith discovered the marks on Charity's neck. Barnabas assures Magda that Charity will keep his secret. Barnabas gives Laura the portrait he found. Sandor finds the grave of Laura Stockbridge who died in 1785. Barnabas demands that the tomb be opened.

EPISODE 524: Laura's coffin is empty. Laura watches Barnabas and Sandor. Laura has Magda burn the portrait. Quentin receives a cablegram confirming a certain incident in Alexandria. Quentin reads it to Laura. It states that Laura died in 1896.

EPISODE 525: Laura laughs at Quentin's statement. Quentin vows that he will learn how she has returned and why. When Quentin leaves the cottage, Dirk enters. Laura makes plans to meet him later. Barnabas goes to Quentin's room and takes his Egyptian Book of the Dead. He uses the book to conjure up the spirit of Laura Stockbridge Collins. The spirit tells Barnabas she has returned in the form of Laura Murdock Collins to take the children. Quentin bursts into the room as the spirit vanishes.

EPISODE 526: Barnabas explains what he did to Quentin, and they decided to join forces. Dirk tells Laura that Jenny is at Collinwood. They formulate a plan to have her kill Quentin. Later, in the basement room, Laura's voice tells Jenny to find Quentin and kill him.

EPISODE 527: Jenny has escaped to the old house. Quentin goes out hunting for her. Barnabas takes her to Josette's room. When dawn comes, Barnabas leaves Jenny and goes to his coffin. Quentin comes to the old house and searches for Jenny.

EPISODE 528: Beth stops Quentin from killing Jenny. Jenny runs from the room to the basement and begins to open Barnabas' coffin.

EPISODE 529: Jenny sees Barnabas inside the coffin. Magda makes her promise not to tell anyone about what she saw. Magda threatens Quentin with a curse if anything happens to Jenny. Magda also admits that Jenny is her sister. Barnabas tries to convince Judith that Jenny could stay with him. Jenny declares (in front of Judith) that she saw Barnabas dead in his coffin.

EPISODE 530: Jenny runs from the old house. Barnabas and Judith return to Collinwood to retrieve her. Barnabas explains to Judith that Jenny's statement about him was in her mad mind. Jenny is hiding in Beth's room. Quentin comes to Beth and confesses his love for her. While they embrace, Jenny comes at them with a large knife.

EPISODE 531: Quentin struggles with Jenny and strangles her. Beth runs downstairs and tells Edward that Quentin killed Jenny by accident. Edward is determined to keep the family from scandal and will tell everybody that Jenny tripped and fell down a flight of stairs. Magda and Sandor come to see Jenny. They find a button clenched in Jenny's fist. Later, Magda discovers a button missing from Quentin's coat. She knows that Quentin killed Jenny and warns him she will put a curse on him.

EPISODE 532: Magda tells Sandor the history of the curse she will put on Quentin. Quentin asks Edward to give him $10,000 to bribe Magda with. Edward gives it to him on the condition that he leave for good. Quentin offers the money to remove the curse before she even puts it on him. Quentin explains that he knows the curse is to have Jenny haunt him. Magda pretends to remove the curse and accepts the money. Sandor offers Quentin a drink to celebrate. After he drinks, Magda gives him his money back and explains she only pretended to take it. She tells him the drink he took contained a potion that will start the curse.

EPISODE 533: Judith tells Beth she is no longer needed. Quentin tells Beth they will leave together. The full moon rises and Magda recites the curse incantation. Quentin feels a sudden pain come over him. Beth runs for a doctor.

EPISODE 534: Beth and Rachel find Beth's room a shambles but no sign of Quentin. Trask learns from Dorcas (a teacher) that Rachel has gone to Collinwood. Trask orders Rachel back to school. Later that evening, Dorcas is attacked by a wild animal. Trask and Rachel find her mangled body.

EPISODE 535: Quentin calls Evan Hanley to help him remove the curse. Evan visits Magda and notices a pentagram around her neck. Evan draws a pentagram on the floor of Quentin's room. He tells Quentin to remain inside the pentagram and he may be cured. Beth comes to see Quentin. The pains begin and he enters the pentagram but changes into a werewolf.

EPISODE 536: Beth steps into the pentagram and it protects her from the werewolf. The werewolf runs off to look for other prey. At the school, Tim brings Jamison (who's locked in a closet for punishment) some food. Charity comes to Jamison and takes his food away. She gives him a book of meditations to read. When she leaves, Jamison escapes. He goes to Collinwood and Beth hides him. Charity and Tim come to Collinwood and are certain to find Jamison. After they do not find him, they leave. Beth realizes Jamison left Collinwood and goes out to search for him. She is confronted by the werewolf in the woods.

EPISODE 537: Barnabas drives the werewolf away with his cane. Jamison is with Laura. Jamison complains to Laura that he feels ill. Barnabas changes into a bat and flies through the cottage window. Barnabas searches for Laura's scarab that contains her life force. Laura catches Barnabas and gets the scarab from him. Laura tries to use her powers against Barnabas but they don't work. Barnabas grabs Jamison and runs off with him. Laura screams after him, vowing revenge.

EPISODE 538: Barnabas returns Jamison to Collinwood. Laura tells Barnabas she will destroy him. Laura sends Dirk to search the old house for letters from the 18th century. Dirk finds the diary of Ben Stokes and brings it to Laura. Laura believes the secret of Barnabas is in Ben's grave. They open it as Barnabas watches.

EPISODE 539: Barnabas takes Ben's diary from Laura. They both vow to destroy each other. Barnabas goes to the school and partakes of Charity's blood. Dirk discovers Barnabas' coffin in the basement. Laura goes to the basement and prepares to drive a stake through Barnabas' heart.

EPISODE 540: Angelique stops Laura. Laura leaves the old house as Magda enters. Angelique orders Magda to bring Quentin to her. Quentin and Angelique plot a way to destroy Laura. Magda steals Laura's scarab for Angelique. Quentin begins an incantation. Laura begins to feel weak and begins to pray to Ra.

EPISODE 541: Jamison has a vision of what is happening to his mother. Jamison goes to the old house. Quentin and Angelique stop their ceremony. Laura prays to Ra for the power to destroy Angelique.

EPISODE 542: Angelique vanishes. Quentin tells Magda what happened. Dirk is attacked by Barnabas. Laura finds Dirk unconscious. Laura runs to Jamison's room only to find a bed of pillows and Angelique laughing at her.

EPISODE 543: Angelique explains her presence to Laura. Laura calls to Nora and Jamison from the fire. Angelique casts a spell to have all the years catch up with her. When Laura appears to the children, they scream, because her face is aged.

EPISODE 544: Barnabas uses his powers to enter the burning room. The flames go out and Edward takes the children to their rooms. Quentin and Evan attempt to contact the devil. A figure appears and Quentin falls to the ground.

EPISODE 545: The dark figure turns out to be Rev. Trask. He has come to discuss the lease for the school yard. Evan explains to him that he and Quentin were playing a game to pass the time. Trask decides to come back another time. Quentin comes to, and Evan explains that the ceremony was ruined by Trask and refuses to try again. Evan drugs Tim and explains that at the right time, he is going to kill someone.

EPISODE 546: Evan sends Tim to Magda to buy some nightshade. Beth begs Magda to end the curse and tells her about Quentin's two children. Magda agrees to help. Tim tries to force Evan to drink the nightshade.

EPISODE 547: Quentin's infant son becomes ill. Barnabas learns that Beth has ordered a silver pentagram. Judith and Beth hears shots from outside and Barnabas rushes in to inform them that the creature has been wounded. He notices Beth's dismayed reaction to the news. Later, he appears in Beth's room demanding to be told who the werewolf is. When she refuses, he attacks her.

EPISODE 548: The now-passive Beth tells Barnabas all about Quentin's curse, the murder of Jenny and about the children. Barnabas explains to Beth that Quentin will not be killed by the ordinary bullets that were fired at him in his other firm. Later, Magda loads her gun with silver bullets and plans to put an end to Quentin's misery. Magda approaches the beast with her gun and fires it. The beast collapses.

EPISODE 549: Barnabas finds Magda standing over the werewolf. They carry him to the old house. If he is kept alive until morning he will live, but the beast jumps up and runs out of the house. Later, Quentin comes to in the woods and returns to Collinwood. Judith informs Barnabas that Jamison had a dream about David Collins.

EPISODE 550: Jamison tells Barnabas about his dream. He described that David dies after his birthday party.

EPISODE 551: Dirk tries to convince Judith that Laura is not dead. Barnabas gives Beth a gun and tells her to guard him during the day. Dirk arrives at the old house the next day, takes the gun from Beth and goes to the basement. Dirk fires the gun at Barnabas over and over again.

EPISODE 552: Dirk locks Beth in the basement with Barnabas. Dirk tells Jamison that Barnabas is dead and that Barnabas was a vampire. That night, Barnabas rises and tells Beth that Dirk did not use silver bullets. Barnabas attacks Dirk in the woods. Barnabas orders Beth to find Jamison and convince him that Dirk was mad when he told his secret, but Jamison has found his coffin.

EPISODE 553: Jamison escapes from the basement before Barnabas finds him. Jamison tells Edward about the coffin. Edward questions Barnabas about the coffin. Barnabas denies everything and shows Edward the now-empty basement. Barnabas has hidden Dirk in the secret room behind the bookcase. When Barnabas goes to the secret room, Dirk is gone.

EPISODE 554: (This episode was shown out of sequence and is now inserted in its' proper place): Barnabas informs Beth that he was going to convince Edward that Dirk is the vampire. Carl returns from Atlantic City with a mentalist, Pansy Faye. Judith agrees to let Pansy perform her act to help find Dirk. During the ceremony, Pansy accuses one of them of killing Dirk. Later, she is attacked by a bat.

EPISODE 555: Barnabas finds Pansy's body and buries her in the woods. Charity breaks her engagement with Tim. Later, Tim pours a drug into Mrs. Trask's tea.

EPISODE 556: A sudden pain strikes Minerva. She collapses and dies. Evan arrives and instructs Tim to forget everything that he has done. Tim plans to hide at Peterson's farm. Tim finds a coffin there and begins to open it.

EPISODE 557: Tim finds the coffin empty but Dirk finds him and attacks him. Judith goes to the old house and finds Dirk. Dirk attacks her and goes back to his hiding place. Rachel comes looking for Tim and Dirk attacks her also.

EPISODE 558: Dirk tells Rachel that she can be a great help to him. Then Dirk appears at Collinwood and renders Edward unconscious. He goes to Judith and tells her he has something important for her to do and hands her a gun. Edward revives and goes to Judith's room, but she is gone. At Peterson's farm, Rachel helps Dirk back into his coffin. Judith comes to the hiding place and aims the loaded gun at Rachel.

EPISODE 559: Tim hears the shots and runs in to find Judith standing over Rachel's body. Tim takes Rachel to the old house where Rachel passes away. Judith returns to Collinwood in a catatonic state. Edward takes the gun away and brings her to her room. Later Dirk rises and calls for Judith. Edward follows Judith to Dirk's hiding place. Judith tries to warn Dirk that Edward has followed her. She faints and Edward drives a stake through Dirk's heart.

EPISODE 560: Judith can remember nothing. She is consoled by Trask. Tim and Carl bury Rachel. Tim leaves. Carl hears Pansy's spirit calling to him. Carl realizes that Pansy is dead.

EPISODE 561: Magda reveals the hand of Count Petofi to Barnabas. She explains how it will lift the curse from Quentin. Pansy comes to Carl in a dream. She sends him a vision of the mausoleum and he realizes that this is where the vampire is.

EPISODE 562: Carl sees Barnabas enter the secret room. Magda tells Quentin about the hand that will cure him. Carl brings Quentin to the secret room. Magda asks Angelique for help. She refuses. Quentin locks Carl in the secret room. Carl figures out how to open the door and escapes.

EPISODE 563: Carl returns to Collinwood and finds Trask to be the only one there. Carl tells Trask about Barnabas. Quentin goes to the secret room and tells Barnabas that Carl knows about him. Barnabas kills Carl and Trask finds the body. Trask goes to the old House and confronts Barnabas with a cross.

EPISODE 564 Barnabas is forced to vanish before Trask's eyes. Trask tells Edward his story and he believes him. Barnabas rises and tells Magda his coffin is now behind the bookcase in the secret room. Edward and Trask search the old house and find the coffin. Trask attaches a cross to it. Barnabas realizes he cannot return to his coffin and goes to Charity for help. He talks her into hiding him at the school. Barnabas sends Charity to the old house to get some soil from his resting place. Edward catches Charity in the old house basement.

Thayer David

David Selby

EPISODE 565: Charity makes excuses that Edward does not believe. Edward finds the marks on her neck and takes her home. Barnabas hides in Charity's room as Edward and Charity enter. Trask leaves Charity to pray. Barnabas comes to Charity and takes her purse filled with the soil that he needs. Then Nora enters as Barnabas bites Charity's neck.

EPISODE 566: Barnabas hypnotized Nora into forgetting about what she saw., then vanishes. At the old house, Barnabas and Magda discuss the hand. Magda screams because the hand is gone. The hand appears in Charity's room. It covers her face and moves to her throat. Evan notices that the marks on her neck are now gone. Even becomes very curious about the hand. Back at the old house, Magda and Barnabas are dismayed when the hand reappears. Barnabas tells Magda to hide the hand. Barnabas returns to his coffin in its new hiding place. Evan is waiting for him there with a cross in his hand.

EPISODE 567: Evan demands to be told of the hand and wants Barnabas to bring it to him by dawn or he will destroy him. Barnabas promises to get the hand for him. Trask proposes to Judith and she accepts. Evan demands the hand and Barnabas warns him that the hand belongs to the evil Count Petofi. Later, Barnabas and Magda hear Evan scream. They find him and his face is grotesquely disfigured.

EPISODE 568: Magda hides Evan in the basement. Quentin discovers Evan and learns that the hand made him that way. He does not want Magda to use the hand to cure him of the curse. Magda changes his mind and begins her incantation.

EPISODE 569: The hand fails to cure Quentin and he transforms into a werewolf. In the woods, Charity is startled by the beast and runs to Collinwood. Magda calms her and brings her to her room. Charity has a dream about Quentin. In the dream, the werewolf appears. She awakes screaming. In the woods, the werewolf steps into a trap, set by one of the deputies.

EPISODE 570: The captured werewolf is placed in the jail. Edward confronts Magda with questions about Barnabas' whereabouts. he tells her about the werewolf's capture. Edward goes to the jail at dawn and watched the transformation.

EPISODE 571: The transformation takes place, but Quentin's face is disfigured and Edward doesn't recognize him. Judith has nightmares about Minerva. Edward is concerned and sends for Evan. Evan arrives with his face back to normal. He goes into the drawing room to see Judith who accuses him of murdering her. She believes she is Minerva Trask and grabs a knife and attacks Evan with it.

EPISODE 572: Edward rushes in and saves Evan. Evan and Trask later plot to drive Judith insane by conjuring up the spirit of Minerva. The spirit appears in the drawing room. Judith runs up the stairs and Minerva follows.

EPISODE 573: Trask follows Judith into her room and insists that Minerva is not there. At the jail cell, Barnabas attacks the guard and frees Quentin. Quentin goes to Collinwood and plays his gramophone. Judith comes in and screams. Quentin tries to talk to her. Minerva's ghost blocks the path out of the room. She is holding a knife, and comes toward Judith.

EPISODE 574: Trask comes in and Quentin runs out the door. Trask denies seeing Minerva. Quentin goes to Evan and demands to see the hand. Quentin knocks Evan out and takes the hand. A stranger arrives and demands the hand be give to him.

EPISODE 575: The stranger is Aristede. he attacks Quentin with a knife and takes the hand form him. Quentin asks Angelique to help him get the hand back Angelique meets Aristede and uses black magic to make him chock.

EPISODE 576: Angelique forces the information about the hand from Aristede. Victor Fenn Gibbons arrives and is welcomed by Edward. Angelique tries to use the hand to change Quentin's face, but she cannot control it and Quentin changes into a werewolf. From the window, Victor Fenn Gibbons is watching.

EPISODE 577: Victor searches the house after the beast and Angelique have left it. He does not find the hand. At the Blue Whale, the Gypsy, Julianka arrives and is questioned by Aristede. He discovers that she is looking for Magda and leads her to the old house. Julianka goes in and meets Barnabas. She informs him that she has come to end the curse placed upon Quentin, but she must have the hand first. In the woods, the werewolf attacks Aristede. He is saved by Victor. The werewolf strangely obeys Victor and is brought to the mill.

EPISODE 578: Quentin, his face restored, is tied to a chair. Aristede unties him and then forces him onto a table beneath a curved blade, then ties him and sets the blade in motion. Barnabas gets the hand from Angelique and gives it to Julianka, who pulls a knife on him. She tells him she tricked him and leaves. In the woods, a bat and then Barnabas appears and puts Julianka under his power. He tells her that she will end Quentin's curse. At the mill, the blade is coming closer to Quentin.

EPISODE 579: Barnabas comes to mill and puts Aristede under his power. Aristede tells him where Quentin is. Barnabas saves Quentin from the blade. Barnabas brings him to the old house and tells Julianka to begin the ceremony to cure Quentin. She tells them that she needs to go and find new block of the orris root to draw the gods to them. She leaves and is later found dead in the woods.

(This episode was skipped by Worldvision Enterprises).

EPISODE 580: After being cursed by the spirit of Julianka, Magda answers the three knocks at the door. It is Sandor with a knife in his back. Barnabas says the body is cold and he has been dead for a long time. Magda later learns that Quentin's son is also dead. Quentin is shocked to learn that he had a son. Magda takes the hand and chops it in two with an axe.

EPISODE 581: Magda tells Quentin she destroyed the hand. Tim is at the window, listening. The hand appears to Magda and she runs from the old house. Tim enters and steals the hand.

EPISODE 582: In the forest, Aristede tells Victor he does not have the hand. They go and search the old house for the hand and they are caught by Magda and Quentin. Victor tells them that he wants the hand. In a struggle with Quentin, Victor's glove slips off, revealing that he has no hand. Magda exclaims that he is Count Petofi!

(This episode has been skipped by Worldvision Enterprises)

EPISODE 583: Quentin informs Edward that Jamison is possessed by Count Petofi. At that moment, Jamison enters and demands a brandy. Edward is shocked and calls for a doctor. Beth takes Jamison to his room. Jamison kisses her and she falls into a mesmerized state. In the drawing room, Edward finds Jamison. Jamison kisses Edward and Edward now believes he is a servant for the Earl of Hampshire.

EPISODE 584: Charles Delaware Tate arrives, and announces that he has been hired to paint a portrait of Quentin. Quentin and Charity bring Edward to the tower room and lock him in. Jamison kisses Charity and she begins to act like Pansy Faye. Barnabas comes out of the secret panel and brings him to the old house.

(This episode has been skipped by Worldvision Enterprises)

EPISODE 585: Charity has read the confession that Trask destroyed. It states that he plotted to kill Minerva. Trask claims that it is a lie. Charity leaves and Trask rips up the confession as Tate enters. Tate asks Trask for a photo of Quentin. Trask gets one out of the drawer and also finds the now restored confession. At Tate's studio, Charity watches him paint the portrait. Tate leaves and she sees the image in the portrait change into a wolf.

EPISODE 586: Hearing Charity scream, Tate runs back and hears Charity's explanation of what she has seen. The portrait, however, is as it was before. They hear the wolf howl and Tate suggests that Charity was imagining things. Jamison pretends that he is no longer possessed by Petofi. Magda lets him out of the cell and he kisses her. Jamison asks her to take him and Aristede to Barnabas' coffin. She agrees.

EPISODE 587: Magda leads them to the coffin but it is empty. Aristede finds the family history book from 1965. He questions Magda and learns that Barnabas is from 1969. In the woods, Charity finds Quentin lying on the ground. A woman's mauled body is nearby. Before she dies, Charity hears her whisper Quentin's name.

EPISODE 588: Charity accuses Quentin of being the werewolf. She promises not to tell anyone, but later she changes her mind and phones the police.

EPISODE 589: Quentin shows Charity her father's confession and tells her that if she tells her father about him, he will tell the police about her father. Mrs. Fillmore tells Quentin that his daughter Lenore has fallen ill. Quentin wants Magda to summon Julianka's spirit. Magda tries, begging Julianka to have mercy on the child. The cradle begins to rock and a figure appears.

EPISODE 590: The figure is not Julianka but Jenny. She sings a lullaby to the baby and tells Quentin the baby will be healthy and well. Trask tells Edward that Quentin is his enemy and that Edward must kill him. Quentin has a dream about Jenny who tells him not to keep their daughter at Collinwood. In the dream, Edward comes in and helps Quentin on with his coat and then begins adjusting his tie. Edward pulls tighter and tighter until Quentin wakes up and finds Edward strangling him.

EPISODE 591: Nora comes in and screams. Edward releases Quentin. Trask takes Edward back to the tower room. At the inn, Tim Shaw looks at the hand before placing it back in its box. Amanda Harris arrives and they embrace. Tim reminds her of their agreement and sends her to Collinwood. Amanda tells Trask about her sinful past and begs for his help. Quentin searches Tim's room but doesn't find the hand. Tim brings the hand (wrapped, in a box) to Nora and tells her to hide it for him. She agrees. After Tim leaves, she tries to open the box but finds it locked.

(This episode has been skipped by Worldvision Enterprises)

EPISODE 592: Jamison leaves Collinwood with the hand. He collapses in the woods, where Quentin finds him semi-conscious. In an attempt to save Jamison, Barnabas brings the hand to the mill and asks to see Petofi. Aristede brings the hand to Petofi. Later, Petofi bursts out of his room with the hand reattached to his wrist.

EPISODE 593: Barnabas wants Petofi's word that Jamison has recovered and that he will remove Quentin's curse. Petofi wants Barnabas to tell him the secret of time travel. Barnabas says he does not even know how to return to his own time. The next day, Petofi forces Magda to take him to Barnabas' Coffin. he then has the coffin chained after placing a cross on Barnabas' chest.

EPISODE 594: Petofi causes Jamison to become possessed by the spirit of David Collins.

EPISODE 595: Quentin goes to Petofi and begs him to save Jamison. Petofi shows him the chained coffin. He allows Quentin to break the chains and speak to Barnabas, who begs Quentin to remove the cross from his chest. Petofi intervenes. later, Beth tries to remove the chains, but Petofi stops her. He then shows her a vision of her becoming a vampire.

EPISODE 596: Charity threatens to tell her father if Petofi doesn't go, but when she tries to speak, she has lost her voice after Petofi touched her throat.

EPISODE 597: Petofi now has Charity under his power. He shows her a vision. She sees Aristede about to be killed by a hooded figure. She then describes her vision of Petofi being tied to a chair and a hooded figure, armed with a scimitar, cuts off his hand. Petofi stops Charity from going any further and tells her she will begin a new life, and she begins acting like Pansy Faye. Magda gets a message from the Gypsies.

EPISODE 598: Magda shows Petofi the note, but he says he knows the Gypsies are coming. Later that night, Magda finds the old house in a shambles and King Johnny Romano there. He demands the hand but Magda tells him she does not have it or know where it is. Then the box appears. He opens it and finds the hand.

EPISODE 599: King Johnny calls Magda a murderer because she can't tell him who killed Julianka. He plans to take her back with him to the tribe where she will be put on trial. In the Gypsy camp, a wind blows and a bearded man appears. The hand floats over the handless figure. Johnny realizes the hand is a fake.

EPISODE 600: Petofi congratulates Tate o his work on the hand he took from a grave to pass off as the real one. He also tells him that he must meet Amanda Harris. Tim explains part of his plan of revenge on Trask. Tate sees Amanda at the inn and is in shock. Later, back at his studio, Tate is staring at the portrait he has been painting and it is of Amanda.

—DARK SHADOWS—

a gallery of dark shadows

Grayson Hall

Jonathan Frid and Alexandra Moltke

Roger Davis and
Kathryn Leigh Scott

Jonathan Frid

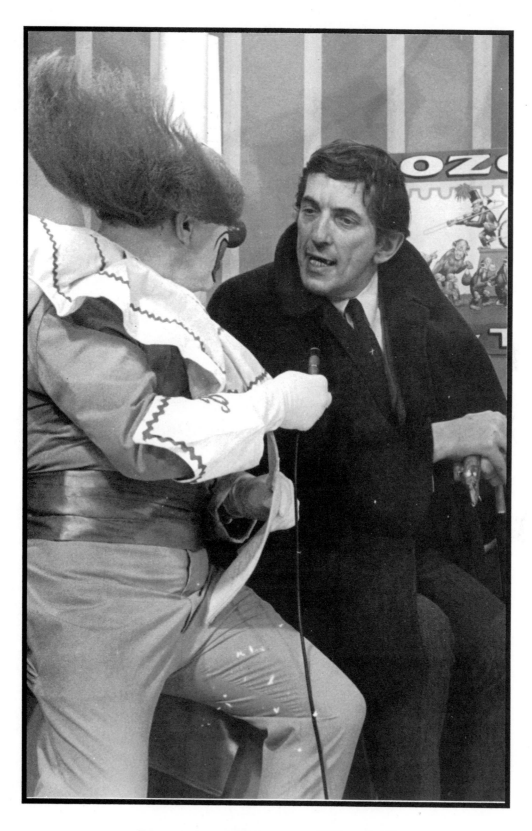

Jonathan Frid
meets Bozo the Clown

*Grayson Hall
and Nanccy Barrett*

David Selby

—DARK SHADOWS—

*Grayson Hall
and David Selby*

—DARK SHADOWS—

*Jonathan Frid, Louis
Edmonds and Joan Bennett*

The World's Only
Official

COUCH
POTATO
BOOK
CATALOG ™

Please note:
You must be a certified couch potato* to partake of this offering!

* To become a certified couch potato you must watch a minimum of 25 hours a day at least 8 days per week.

From Happy Hal...

Star Trek
Gunsmoke
The Man from U.N.C.L.E.

They all evoke golden memories of lost days of decades past. What were you doing when you first saw them?

Were you sitting with your parents and brothers and sisters gathered around a small set in your living room?

Were you in your own apartment just setting out on the wonders of supporting yourself, with all of the many associated fears?

Or were you off at some golden summer camp with all of the associated memories, of course forgetting the plague of mosquitoes and the long, arduous hikes?

The memories of the television show are mixed with the memories of the time in a magical blend that always brings a smile to your face. Hopefully we can help bring some of the smiles to life, lighting up your eyes and heart with our work...

Look inside at the **UNCLE Technical Manual**, the **Star Trek Encyclopedia, The Compleat Lost in Space** or the many, many other books about your favorite television shows!

Let me know what you think of our books.

And what you want to see.

It's the only way we can share our love of the wonders of the magic box....

Selection
HAL SCHUSTER
Administration
JACK SCHUSTER, COUCH POTATO
Customer Service
PHYLLIS SCHUSTER

From The Couch Potato...

I am here working hard on your orders.

Let me tell you about a few new things we have added to help speed up your order. First we are computerizing the way we process your order so that we can more easily look it up if we need to and maintain our customer list. The program will also help us process our shipping information by including weight, location and ordering information which will be essential if you have a question or complaint (Heavens Forbid).

We are now using UPS more than the post office. This helps in many ways including tracing a package if it is lost and in more speedily getting your package to you because they are quicker. . They are also more careful with shipments and they arrive in better condition. UPS costs a little more than post office, This is unfortunate but we feel you will find that it is worth it.

Also please note our new discount program. Discounts range from 5% to 20% off.

So things are looking up in 1988 for Coach Potato.

I really appreciate your orders and time but I really must get back to the tube...

The Phantom
The Green Hornet
The Shadow
The Batman

Each issue of Serials Adventures Presents offers 100 or more pages of pure nostalgic fun for $16.95

Flash Gordon Part One
Flash Gordon Part Two
Blackhawk

Each issue of Serials Adventures Presents features a chapter by chapter review of a rare serial combined with biographies of the stars and behind-the-scenes information. Plus rare photos. See the videotapes and read the books!

THE U.N.C.L.E. TECHNICAL MANUAL

Every technical device completely detailed and blueprinted, including weapons, communications, weaponry, organization, facitilites... 80 pages. 2 volumes...$9.95 each

NUMBER SIX: THE COMPLEAT PRISONER

The most unique and intelligent television series ever aired! Patrick McGoohan's tour-de-force of spies and mental mazes finally explained episode by episode, including an interview with the McGoohan and the complete layout of the real village!...160 pages...$14.95

THE GREEN HORNET

Daring action adventure with the Green Hornet and Kato. This show appeared before Bruce Lee had achieved popularity but delivered fun, superheroic action. Episode guide and character profiles combine to tell the whole story...120 pages...$14.95

WILD, WILD, WEST

Is it a Western or a Spy show? We couldn't decide so we're listing it twice. Fantastic adventure, convoluted plots, incredible devices...all set in the wild, wild west! Details of fantastic devices, character profiles and an episode-by-episode guide...120 pages...$17.95

THE FREDDY KRUEGER STORY

The making of the monster. Including interviews with director Wes Craven and star Robert Englund. Plus an interview with Freddy himself! $14.95

THE ALIENS STORY

Interviews with movie director James Cameron, stars Sigourney Weaver and Michael Biehn and effects people and designers Ron Cobb, Syd Mead, Doug Beswick and lots more!...$14.95

ROBOCOP

Law enforcement in the future. Includes interviews with the stars, the director, the writer, the special effects people, the storyboard artists and the makeup men! $16.95

MONSTERLAND'S HORROR IN THE '80s

The definitive book of the horror films of the '80s. Includes interviews with the stars and makers of Aliens, Freddy Krueger, Robocop, Predator, Fright Night, Terminator and all the others! $17.95

LOST IN SPACE

THE COMPLEAT LOST IN SPACE
244 PAGES...$17.95
TRIBUTE BOOK
Interviews with everyone!...$7.95
TECH MANUAL
Technical diagrams to all of the special ships and devices plus exclusive production artwork....$9.95

GERRY ANDERSON

SUPERMARIONATION
Episode guides and character profiles to Capt Scarlet, Stingray, Fireball, Thunderbirds, Supercar and more...240 pages...$17.95

BEAUTY AND THE BEAST

THE UNOFFICIAL BEAUTY&BEAST
Complete first season guide including interviews and biographies of the stars. 132 pages $14.95

DARK SHADOWS

DARK SHADOWS TRIBUTE BOOK
Interviews, scripts and more... 160 pages...$14.95

DARK SHADOWS INTERVIEWS BOOK
A special book interviewing the entire cast. $18.95

DOCTOR WHO THE BAKER YEARS

A complete guide to Tom Baker's seasons as the Doctor including an in-depth episode guide, interviews with the companions and profiles of the characters... 300 pages...$19.95

THE DOCTOR WHO ENCYCLOPEDIA: THE FOURTH DOCTOR

Encyclopedia of every character, villain and monster of the Baker Years. ..240 pages...$19.95

THE COUCH POTATO BOOK CATALOG 5715 N BALSAM, LAS VEGAS, NV 89130

THE ILLUSTRATED STEPHEN KING

A complee guide to the novels and short stories of Stephen King illustrated by Steve Bissette and others...$12.95

GUNSMOKE YEARS

The definitive book of America's most successful television series. 22 years of episode guide, character profiles, interviews and more...240 pages, $14.95

THE REST OF THE SHOW

THE KING COMIC HEROES

The complete story of the King Features heroes including Prince Valiant, Flash Gordon, Mandrake, The Phantom, Secret Agent, Rip Kirby, Buz Sawyer, Johnny Hazard and Jungle Jim. These fabulous heroes not only appeared in comic strips and comic books but also in movies and serials. Includes interviews with Hal Foster, Al Williamson and Lee Falk...$14.95

Special discounts are available for library, school, club or other bulk orders. Please inquire.

IF YOUR FAVORITE TELEVISION SERIES ISN'T HERE, LET US KNOW...
AND THEN STAY TUNED!

And always remember that if every world leader was a couch potato and watched TV 25 hours a day, 8 days a week, there would be no war...

THE COUCH POTATO BOOK CATALOG 5715 N BALSAM, LAS VEGAS, NV 89130

Boring, but Necessary Ordering Information!

Payment: All orders must be prepaid by check or money order. Do not send cash. All payments must be made in US funds only.

Shipping: We offer several methods of shipment for our product.

Postage is as follows:

For books priced under $10.00— for the first book add $2.50. For each additional book under $10.00 add $1.00. (This is per individual book priced under $10.00, not the order total.)

For books priced over $10.00— for the first book add $3.25. For each additional book over $10.00 add $2.00. (This is per individual book priced over $10.00, not the order total.)

These orders are filled as quickly as possible. Sometimes a book can be delayed if we are temporarily out of stock. You should note on your order whether you prefer us to ship the book as soon as available or send you a merchandise credit good for other TV goodies or send you your money back immediately. Shipments normally take 2 or 3 weeks, but allow up to 12 weeks for delivery.

Special UPS 2 Day Blue Label RUSH SERVICE: Special service is available for desperate Couch Potatos. These books are shipped within 24 hours of when we receive your order and should take 2 days to get from us to you.

For the first **RUSH SERVICE** book under $10.00 add $4.00. For each additional l book under $10.00 and $1.25. (This is per individual book priced under $10.00, not the order total.)

For the first **RUSH SERVICE** book over $10.00 add $6.00. For each additional book over $10.00 add $3.50 per book. (This is per individual book priced over $10.00, not the order total.)

Canadian and Foreign shipping rates are the same except that Blue Label RUSH SERVICE is not available. All Canadian and Foreign orders are shipped as books or printed matter.

DISCOUNTS! DISCOUNTS! Because your orders are what keep us in business we offer a discount to people that buy a lot of our books as our way of saying thanks. On orders over $25.00 we give a 5% discount. On orders over $50.00 we give a 10% discount. On orders over $100.00 we give a 15% discount. On orders over $150.00 we give a 20% discount. Please list alternates when possible. Please state if you wish a refund or for us to backorder an item if it is not in stock.

100% satisfaction guaranteed. We value your support. You will receive a full refund as long as the copy of the book you are not happy with is received back by us in reasonable condition. No questions asked, except we would like to know how we failed you. Refunds and credits are given as soon as we receive back the item you do not want.

Please have mercy on Phyllis and carefully fill out this form in the neatest way you can. Remember, she has to read a lot of them every day and she wants to get it right and keep you happy! You may use a duplicate of this order blank as long as it is clear. **Please don't forget to include payment! And remember, we *love* repeat friends...**

■■■■■■■■■■■■■■■■■■■■■■■**ORDER FORM**■■■■■■■■■■■■■■■■■■■■■■■■■■■■■■■■

_____The Phantom $16.95
_____The Green Hornet $16.95
_____The Shadow $16.95
_____Flash Gordon Part One $16.95_____Part Two $16.95
_____Blackhawk $16.95
_____Batman $16.95
_____The UNCLE Technical Manual One $9.95 _____Two $9.95
_____The Green Hornet Television Book $14.95
_____Number Six The Prisoner Book $14.95
_____The Wild Wild West $17.95
_____Trek Year One $10.95
_____Trek Year Two $12.95
_____Trek Year Three $12.95
_____The Animated Trek $14.95
_____The Movies $12.95
_____Next Generation $19.95
_____The Lost Years $14.95
_____The Trek Encyclopedia $19.95
_____Interviews Aboard The Enterprise $18.95
_____The Ultimate Trek $75.00
_____Trek Handbook $12.95_____Trek Universe $17.95
_____The Crew Book $17.95
_____The Making of the Next Generation $14.95
_____The Freddy Krueger Story $14.95
_____The Aliens Story $14.95
_____Robocop $16.95
_____Monsterland's Horror in the '80s $17.95
_____The Compleat Lost in Space $17.95
_____Lost in Space Tribute Book $9.95
_____Lost in Space Tech Manual $9.95
_____Supermarionation $17.95
_____The Unofficial Beauty and the Beast $14.95
_____Dark Shadows Tribute Book $14.95
_____Dark Shadows Interview Book $18.95
_____Doctor Who Baker Years $19.95
_____The Doctor Who Encyclopedia:The 4th Doctor $19.95
_____Illustrated Stephen King $12.95
_____Gunsmoke Years $14.95

NAME:_____

STREET:_____

CITY:_____

STATE:_____

ZIP:_____

TOTAL:_____ SHIPPING_____

SEND TO: COUCH POTATO,INC.
5715 N BALSAM, LAS VEGAS, NV 89130